GROUND WAR – VIETNAM

VOL. 2
1965-1968

By Jim Mesko
Color by Don Greer

squadron/signal publication

Marine infantry, supported by tanks and H-34 helicopters, engage the Viet Cong during Operation STARLIGHT conducted near Chu Lai in August of 1965.

ISBN 0-89747-288-8

If you have any photographs of the aircraft, armor, soldiers or ships of any nation, particularly wartime snapshots, why not share them with us and help make Squadron/Signal's books all the more interesting and complete in the future. Any photograph sent to us will be copied and the original returned. The donor will be fully credited for any photos used. Please send them to:

Squadron/Signal Publications, Inc.
1115 Crowley Drive.
Carrollton, TX 75011-5010.

Dedication

To all the Americans who fought in Vietnam, but especially for those who died or still remain there as MIAs and to the memory of "Bonz" who brought happiness to all who knew him.

A special thanks must go to four teachers who helped develop my interest in history and writing: Fritz Paolino, Mae Packn, Sally Miller and Doctor David Riede. Without these individuals this book would not have been possible.

Acknowledgments

U.S. Army   U.S. Navy
U.S. Air Force   U.S. Marine Corps
Dana Bell   Terry Love
Stella and Peter Mesko   Patricia Mesko
Bob Krenkel   Reuben Garcia

Introduction

This second volume of Ground War Vietnam deals with a relatively short time span, from the Summer of 1965 to early 1968. This time frame, however, was perhaps the most critical of the entire war, for during these years the United States and its allies made a massive commitment of men and material to forestall a communist victory in Vietnam. Militarily, the goal was achieved, yet by the end of 1968, the Communists had achieved a political victory which undermined the battlefield achievements of the U.S. and its allies. For Vietnam, unlike any other war in America's past, was a political war, something which American leaders, both civil and military, failed (for the most part) to grasp.

Ironically, the micro-management of the war by the self-serving politicians in Washington, worked right into the hands of the North Vietnamese. This rigid control of the war by the politicians, along with the misguided goals which some top military men fostered on the units in-country, set the stage for the final fall of South Vietnam in 1975.

This period of the war encompassed the two most controversial battles of the war, the siege at Khe Sanh and the Tet Offensive. Both, although military victories, were depicted by the news media as defeats. This further helped the enemy achieve their political goals. Interestingly enough, the opening battles of this volume, Operation STARLIGHT and the Ia Drang Valley campaign, both received favorable coverage by the press, yet by 1968 this same media would be considered by many in the military to be their second worst enemy.

Unfortunately during these three years, the early conviction that we were fighting a crusade against communism had slowly but surely been eroded by a multitude of events until cynicism had become the watchword. No one single event, person, or action could be blamed for this outlook, yet as the war dragged on and the numbers of the dead increased, the public grew tired and the very goals being sought were soon under question. This same thing had occurred during the latter days of the Korean War and this was what the communist leadership in Hanoi had hoped for. Eventually this would lead to the American withdrawal in the early 1970s.

In this second installment, the early euphoria of these first victories is shown, along with the tremendous buildup of American and allied power. As the ground war widened, the drudgery that typifies war began to take hold, a rather subtle shift, but nevertheless one which gradually came to pass as the war became a part of our daily lives, until the shock of the Tet Offensive hit the news with a thunderclap, reawakening America to the war which her troops fought daily against a dangerous foe. No period of the Vietnam War saw more change, controversy and shifting of individual positions then during these years.

This then, is the story of the most critical years of the U.S involvement in Vietnam. And while it encompasses the follies and errors of the various leaders, it also portrays the heroism and dedication to duty of the Soldiers, Sailors, Airmen and Marines who fought for their country and against the threat of communism.

First Blood

By the early Summer of 1965, American units were finally freed to seek out enemy forces under the new rules of engagement given to the commander of U.S. troops in Vietnam, GEN William Westmoreland. Aside from a few minor skirmishes with U.S. patrols and some probes against base defenses, however, no significant contact was made throughout June and July. By August, American units were chafing at the bit to bring the elusive enemy into battle.

Finally on 15 August, a deserter from the 1st Viet Cong (VC) Regiment informed the Army of the Republic of Vietnam (ARVN) and Marine forces at Da Nang of a surprise attack planned by his unit against the new Marine base at Chu Lai, south of Da Nang. Moving quickly to forestall this attack, the Marines immediately mounted a three pronged amphibious-ground-air assault against this VC force in the hopes of trapping it against the sea near the village complex of Van Truong.

Operation STARLIGHT began on 17 August, when a Marine company pushed south toward the village from Chu Lai. This did not arouse any suspicion since the Marines had patrolled in this area before. The next day a Marine battalion launched an amphibious assault against a beach south of Van Truong while three companies were dropped off at landing zones (LZs) west of the village. These moves trapped the VC regiment with its back to the sea where Navy ships barred any possible escape by water. One Marine company landed in the middle of a VC battalion, but despite heavy fire, managed to secure the key terrain feature with air, artillery and tank support. Another company, at the village of Ap Cuong 2, sustained heavy casualties and a small group of tanks and amphibious tractors (Amtracs) were sent to relieve them. The column lost its way in the dense jungle, however, and stumbled into a VC ambush. Pinned down, it was finally relieved by the force it was sent to help, backed by massive fire support.

Following this fierce fighting on the first day of STARLIGHT, the VC tried to disengage. For the next week all the Marines ran into were small units trying to cover the withdrawal of the main force. Constant action by air and artillery support took its toll of the enemy and when the operation was terminated (after a week) nearly 700 VC were claimed as killed, nearly 600 by actual body count, along with countless wounded. Marine losses were much less, with 50 killed

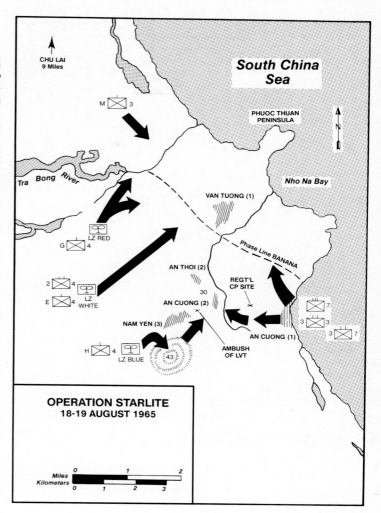

OPERATION STARLITE
18-19 AUGUST 1965

Marines wait to board a H-34 that will take them into the field during Operation STARLIGHT, the first major contact between American and enemy forces in the Vietnam War. The H-34 would serve with the Marines until August of 1969, although it became less common as newer CH-46s and CH-53s arrived in Marine helicopter units. (Sikorsky)

Amphibious tractors (Amtracs) move off the beach through a wooded area during Operation STARLIGHT. The amtracs were eventually found to be unsuited for prolonged use ashore and were susceptible to mines which would set off their fuel tanks located under the floor. During the operation, a column of these vehicles was ambushed by the VC, highlighting the need for armored forces to be supported by infantry. (USMC)

and 200 wounded. Many of these wounded would eventually return to their units.

The command group of the 2nd Battalion, 4th Marines moves up through a village during the initial stages of Operation STARLIGHT, the first major Marine action against the VC. (USMC)

The significance of Operation STARLIGHT was not in its favorable kill ratio, but rather that for the first time in the war, an enemy ground unit had stood toe to toe with an American force and slugged it out. The Marine victory was of great psychological importance since it showed U.S. troops could defeat the enemy on his own ground. Had the Marines been beaten, the backlash from this defeat would have been devastating for both the U.S. forces and ARVN troops while raising VC morale tremendously. As it turned out just the reverse was true and it would be many months before the VC would again actively seek contact with a large Marine force.

An M50 Ontos (Greek word meaning the "Thing") patrols along a beach as the Marines expand their initial landing site during Operation STARLIGHT. The Ontos was a lightly armored vehicle which mounted six 106MM recoilless rifles. (USMC)

A H-34 of HMM-361 hoists a sling load of supplies for Marines conducting Operation STARLIGHT. The ability to resupply troops in the field by helicopters made it possible to keep troops in the field for long periods and lessened the chances for the enemy to interdict Marine supply lines. (USMC)

The Marine commander in Vietnam during Operation STARLIGHT was the legendary Gen Lewis Walt. Gen Walt, briefing a group of marines shortly after taking command, was later caught in the middle of the strategy dispute between Westmoreland and Marine Corps Commandant GEN Wallace Greene and Fleet Marine Force Commander, GEN Victor Krulak. (USMC)

Troops from Company E, 2nd Battalion, 4th Marines move out of LZ White in search of the VC. A short time later the Marines encountered stiff resistance from dug-in guerrillas and a major firefight erupted. Eventually, Operation STARLIGHT resulted in a major Marine victory, the first for U.S. forces in Vietnam. (USMC)

Buildup

With the approval of Washington to expand the scope of U.S. ground operations in Vietnam, GEN Westmoreland decided to use the American and allied troops under his command to attack major enemy units, while employing ARVN troops in the heavily populated areas around the cities and the Mekong Delta. This strategy was chosen because it allowed the more mobile American forces to seek out the enemy in remote areas where heavy firepower could be brought to bear without fear of excessive civilian casualties. This plan also took advantage of the ARVN's knowledge of their own people and local conditions, which were their strong points for the pacification work which was vital if a long term solution was to be found to improve the government's position among the civilian populace.

To carry out his goals, GEN Westmoreland asked for and received additional U.S. troops to supplement the Marines and airborne troops already in-country. Elements of the 1st Infantry Division and 101st Airborne started deployment in late Summer. To supplement the Australian and New Zealand contingents which had arrived in mid-Summer, the Republic of Korea (ROK) sent the 2nd Marine Brigade and Capital Division as their contribution to the allied war effort. These units arrived in the early Fall. At the same time the 1st Cavalry (Airmobile) began unloading its helicopters and equipment and prepared to move into the Central Highlands area. With these forces, Westmoreland had over 175,000 troops under his command (although not all were combat troops) along with the allied and ARVN troops. He planned to use these to basically hold the line and disrupt any detected enemy moves but he also indicated another 100,000 men would be needed to effectively go on the offensive.

Early Moves

The arrival of the 1st Cavalry Division gave GEN Westmoreland a unique tool with which to fight the VC. Being almost totally airmobile through its complement of helicopters, the 1st CAV provided him with a very mobile force which could move against enemy units in very short order.

When its first units arrived in-country during September, he decided to move the Division into the Central Highlands to counter a growing North Vietnamese Army (NVA) threat there. After a survey of the available areas, it was decided to base the unit at the small town of An Khe, midway along Route 19, which ran between Pleiku in the

The decision to build up U.S. strength in Vietnam resulted in a massive influx of troops into the country during the Summer and Fall of 1965. Elements of the 1st Infantry Division rest onboard a ship as they await their arrival off the shore of Vietnam. The long sea voyage for the troops was very boring and was compounded by the fear of what awaited them on their arrival in-country. (Army)

highlands and Qui Nhon on the coast. As the first units moved into the area to set up a base, the 173rd Airborne began a clearing operation, named Operation GIBRALTER, to protect the 1st CAV from communist attack.

GIBRALTER proved to be far more successful then an earlier sweep of the area during June. In three days of operations around An Khe, the paratroopers killed 226 enemy soldiers while losing only a few men to enemy action. Upon the termination of Operation GIBRALTER, the 173rd pulled back to Bien Hoa, leaving base security in the hands of the Cavalrymen. Although they started to immediately patrol around their base, there were few contacts. The local VC were still suffering from their combat with the 173rd and avoided contact, which proved frustrating to the American troops. Events further west, however, were to provide a catalyst which would set off the first large scale battle between U.S. and NVA forces of the war.

Into the Ia Drang Valley

In the Fall of 1965 the communist forces in the Central Highlands began a drive to cut South Vietnam in half. Three NVA regiments, the 32nd, 33rd and 66th moved to attack the Special Forces camp at Plei Me, southwest of Pleiku, a key city in the region. Once the initial assault (by the 33rd) began, they anticipated that the ARVN Commander at Pleiku would commit his only reserves to relieve the besieged camp. With this in mind the other two NVA regiments prepared a massive ambush along the relief route in order to trap and destroy this force. Once this was accomplished, the three regiments would unite and take Pleiku, then proceed down Route 19 to the coast to cut the country in half.

Although not aware of this plan, GEN Westmoreland knew something was up and moved up units of the newly arrived 1st Calvary Division (Airmobile) to support the relief column. When the NVA hit the column in two places, artillery and air strikes helped repulse the attacks, enabling the force to reach and relieve Plei Me. In conjunction with this move, other Air Cav units were brought in around the camp to provide additional artillery support to the defenders. Under such a concentration of fire the NVA abandoned the siege and began a general retreat toward Cambodia.

As things grew quiet around Plei Me, GEN Westmoreland realized the communists were trying to slip away and ordered a general pursuit by the 1st Brigade of the 1st Cav. Throughout October little contact was made with the enemy but on 1 November, a hospital complex was discovered in the Ia Drang Valley. More troops were airlifted in by helicopter as NVA resistance increased, but the enemy was unable to assemble enough manpower to overrun the American troops. Captured documents further revealed communist plans and provided useful intelligence on troop movements which allowed Air Cav units to find and engage them.

On 14 November, during an insertion below the Chu Pong Mountains at LZ X-Ray, a company from the 1st Battalion, 7th Calvary drew heavy fire as it moved out from the LZ. As it pulled back, the NVA began to pound the area with rocket and mortar fire. The battalion commander tried to bring in the rest of the battalion but intense ground fire hindered this and only part of the unit was able to get in. Throughout the day the enemy made several attacks but was unable to break through the defenses. As nightfall approached additional reinforcements and supplies were finally able to get into the LZ as enemy fire slackened off. Numerous NVA probes were made that night but no major attacks occurred. Early the next morning, however, the NVA launched a series of attacks against the perimeter and a call went out for reinforcements. Heavy ground fire drove off not only the reinforcement flight but also the medivac choppers and it was not until late in the morning that the LZ was finally safe for the arriving helicopters.

While the majority of the fighting took place around LZ X-Ray, other Air Cav units were dropped around the general area and began pushing toward the surrounded battalion. Supported by heavy air and artillery fire, the force at the LZ began to push out of the landing zone to link up with other units. The NVA, due to this heavy fire and their own losses, were unable to stop them and gradually broke off contact. By the next day, 16 November, the enemy was in full retreat toward Cambodia with Air Cav units in hot pursuit. Fighting continued until the end of the month, by which time what remained of the three NVA regiments were finally able to reach their sanctuaries in "neutral" Cambodia. By this time, they were combat ineffective, having lost over 1,800 dead plus scores of wounded. Over 240 Americans were also lost, but the green U.S. troops had performed well against the experienced NVA regulars.

Like the Marine victory at Chu Lai, the 1st Cav's impressive performance in the Ia Drang Valley was of great importance. Had the NVA inflicted a telling defeat on the American troops, this would have had a great psychological impact on both U.S. and ARVN forces. Additionally, the battle validated the airmobile concept, until this time only an untested theory. With this victory allied morale soared while the enemy's dropped. But while the immediate threat to the Central Highlands was turned back by this action, the NVA would return again to the area from their sanctuary in Cambodia, a pattern which would become all too common for the rest of the war.

Strategy

With the commitment of American ground forces an established fact, the need arose to devise a strategy for their employment which would lead to a successful conclusion of the war within the shortest possible time. GEN Westmoreland decided that the goal should be the elimination of the hard core VC units and regular NVA troops in Vietnam by means of a war of attrition. Under this concept U.S. forces would seek out the enemy wherever they were and inflict maximum casualties on them through maneuver and superior firepower.

Under this strategy, success on the battlefield would be determined by the number of enemy dead or "body count." Little importance was attached to anything else since the enemy had no major towns under their control, or other obvious targets, which might have had significance in a conventional war. GEN Westmoreland felt that this course of action would force the Communist leadership to eventually realize the futility of their actions and cease their aggression.

This strategy was questioned, however, by the Marine commanders whose troops were located up north in I Corps. The Marines had been the only service to develop a pacification strategy which was based on practical experience. This had come about due to their involvement in numerous small wars in the 1920s and 1930s in the Caribbean and Central American areas. With this background, the Marine Corps commandant, GEN Wallace Greene and GEN Victory Krulak, Commander, Fleet Marine Force, Pacific (FMFPAC) felt that the best way to use the Marines was for pacification rather then offensive sweeps. If used in this way, they felt significant economic and political improvements could be made which would increase support from the peasants and strengthen the Saigon government while under-cutting the communists. Although the emphasis would be placed on this approach, main force enemy units would not be ignored. Rather, they would be tracked by every possible means available, then engaged whenever the situation arose where American forces had a definite advantage. This ran counter to Westmoreland's war of attrition, which called for U.S. troops to be constantly on the attack.

The overall commander of Marine forces in Vietnam, GEN Lewis Walt, tried to implement the Marine strategy. Initially, he achieved a certain degree of success at carrying this out by splitting up the time in the field between pacification and seeking out hard core units on favorable terms to his forces. Unfortunately, Westmoreland did not agree with this approach and began to pressure Walt to shift over to the strategy of attrition. Despite the real success which the Marine pacification program began to experience, as opposed to the apparent success the Army was experiencing with their "body count" approach, Westmoreland slowly forced the Marines away from the populated regions where they had begun making inroads

One of the major units which arrived in-country during this period was the 1st Cavalry (Airmobile). This unit was specifically tailored to fight in Vietnam using helicopters. The helicopter gave it great mobility and much was expected of it. These Cavalrymen unload a truck at Nha Trang wearing the older style Army uniform and jump boots instead of the new jungle fatigues and jungle boots which were in short supply at the time. (Army)

In addition to American units, other Asian allies also provided troops to aid South Vietnam. GEN Westmoreland welcomes a contingent of South Korean Marines to Vietnam at Phan Rang during September of 1965.

South Korean troops from the Capital Division (Tigers) fire a 4.2 inch mortar at VC positions. Eventually the Korean contingent would consist of the Capital and 9th Divisions, the 2nd Marine Brigade and numerous support units.

7

An Australian gun crew sets up their 105MM howitzer at Phan Rang during the Fall of 1965. Until mid-1966, the Australians worked in conjunction with American forces but after that time their strength was increased and a separate Australian Task Force (ATF) was set up. (Army)

This early buildup has its problem. The port facilities available in Vietnam were not able to handle the large amounts of men and material which arrived daily. To alleviate this problem numerous methods were tried to get things ashore, such as these LARC-V, one of which became stuck in the sand at Cam Ranh Bay. This area would later become the largest port for supplies coming into the country. (Army)

In addition to ground and logistical units, two HAWK anti-aircraft missile battalions were also deployed to guard against a possible enemy aerial attack. This HAWK of the 6th Battalion, 71st Artillery is positioned on a sand dune at Cam Ranh Bay. (Army)

into the VC infrastructure by eliminating the cadres and the guerrilla's hold on the peasants.

Little support for the Marine policy was forthcoming from Washington where this approach was felt to be too time consuming. Additionally, there was no easily visible measure of success as was possible with the "body count" approach. Coupled with this was the confidence President Johnson had in Westmoreland and, at this relatively early stage of American participation in the war, what "Westy" wanted, he basically got. With little or no outside support for their policy, the Marines were eventually forced into the war of attrition with the NVA. Orders for offensive operations came out of "Pentagon West," the nickname for Westmorland's headquarters in Saigon and pacification was put on the backburner, eventually to become only a minor portion of the Marine Corps effort in Vietnam.

Following Up

Taking advantage of the momentum gained by Operation STAR-LIGHT, the Marines launched a series of ground sweeps and amphibious assaults to keep the VC off balance. In conjunction with Vietnamese Marines, a combined amphibious/helicopter assault on the Batangan Peninsula destroyed a large VC force during Operation PIRANHA in early September. At the end of the month a similar assault, Operation DAGGER THRUST I, was made against a peninsula south of Qui Nhon in II Corps. This operation destroyed numerous bunkers and tunnel complexes. This was but the first in a series of raids along the coast aimed at destroying enemy positions. Further DAGGER THRUST operations led to some heavy contact with VC units but the Marines suffered only light casualties against heavy enemy losses.

In addition to these amphibious assaults, numerous ground sweeps were mounted but the VC, still reeling from the effects of STARLIGHT, avoided any large scale action. As part of their effort to win over the Vietnamese peasants, the Marines provided security during the rice harvest under Operation GOLDEN FLEECE, denying the VC of a large portion of their expected food supply. In other actions the only contact the Marines ran into were snipers, booby traps and small ambushes, which, though insignificant in the overall picture, were still none the less deadly. During one such incident on Operation BLACK FERRET south of Chu Lai, the famous woman war correspondent, Dickie Chapelle was killed by a booby trap.

The most significant actions in the latter part of 1965 were serveral VC sapper attacks (one against Da Nang and another against Chu Lai), Operation HARVEST MOON and the relief of ARVN troops at Heip Duc and Thach Tru by Marine aviation and ground elements. In the sapper attacks against the two bases, twenty-one helicopters and aircraft were destroyed, although most of the enemy troops were killed by security elements. Operation HARVEST MOON, a combined USMC/ARVN ground sweep between Da Nang and Chu Lai, netted over 400 VC killed against fifty Marine dead. In addition, large quantities of rice and other military supplies were captured or destroyed, dealing the guerrillas in the area a severe logistical set back. At Heip Duc, Marine helicopters, heavily supported by Marine fixed wing aircraft, flew in ARVN reinforcements to help push back a large VC attack, while at Thach Tru, a Marine battalion was rushed in to relieve an Army Ranger battalion under siege by a VC regiment. In both cases, air support played a vital role and forced the VC to break off contact before heavy ground fighting could develop. As the year closed, the Marines had made significant inroads into enemy strength and had caused serious losses to the Viet Cong in men and material.

(Above) Following the Marine victory during Operation STARLIGHT, MACV expanded the scope of U.S. operations in an attempt to bring the enemy to battle. Troops from the 173rd Airborne unload from a Huey during an insertion near Pleiku. By this point in the war the UH-1s had discarded their high visibility markings and carried subdued markings. (Army)

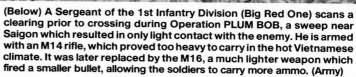

(Below) A Sergeant of the 1st Infantry Division (Big Red One) scans a clearing prior to crossing during Operation PLUM BOB, a sweep near Saigon which resulted in only light contact with the enemy. He is armed with an M14 rifle, which proved too heavy to carry in the hot Vietnamese climate. It was later replaced by the M16, a much lighter weapon which fired a smaller bullet, allowing the soldiers to carry more ammo. (Army)

(Above) Elements from the 1st Infantry Division prepare to set up a perimeter during a sweep near Bien Hoa. The officer pointing wears the early style jungle fatigue shirt while the others have on the older uniform which was too heavy for Vietnam. The soldiers on the left carry M3 Grease Guns which were more widely used in the early days of the war. Its limited range and tendency to jam when the magazine spring rusted led to its replacement by the M14 and (later) M16. (Army)

Troops from the 173rd search the dense jungle in the Central Highlands for signs of the enemy. The dense jungle provided excellent cover for the VC and NVA troops and normally the only way to make contact was for troops to go into the bush and flush them out. (Army)

Artillerymen of the 173rd Airborne fire in support of the 173rd's ground sweep just north of Bien Hoa. They are using an M101A1 105mm howitzer; this weapon was later replaced by the improved M102 which was lighter and had a slightly greater range. (Army)

The terrain in Vietnam varied from region to region. These airborne troops ford a steam on a makeshift log bridge northeast of Saigon. At times like this a unit was especially vulnerable to a VC ambush. (Army)

While large numbers of U.S. combat troops were employed in sweeps against the enemy, Green Beret A Teams still worked with the Monta-guards in the Central Highlands to deny this vital area to the com-munists and hinder their supply lines into South Vietnam. Many of their camps, such as this one at Cia Vuc, relied on aerial resupply by trans-ports such as this C-123 to exist. (Army)

This broad savannah type plain made an ideal landing zone. Unfortunately, the enemy was well aware of these potential LZs and often guarded them with heavy machine guns. This soldier is equipped with an M16 rifle, which early in the war got a lot of bad press due to jamming. After changes were made, the weapon performed well but still required constant care and cleaning. (Army)

It was the efforts on the part of the NVA to dislodge the Special Forces camp at Plei Me, in the Highlands, which led to the first battle of the war between American and NVA regular forces. Elements of the 1st Cav prepare to move out in search of communist forces in the Ia Drang Valley. (Army)

During one of the sweeps an NVA hospital was uncovered, leading to a short but intense firefight. This Sergeant Major examines some of the medical equipment discovered in the complex. Interestingly, while his division patch appears to be subdued, his stripes stand out, which allows for easy detection in the jungle. (Army)

With the realization that major enemy elements were in the area, GEN Westmoreland ordered more troops from the 1st Cav into the region to search for them. These cavalrymen move into a small valley in search of the elusive North Vietnamese. (Army)

During many of the sweeps near populated areas, numerous suspects, who either acted suspiciously or did not have the proper papers, were taken prisoner and handed over to the South Vietnamese for questioning. A Military Policeman (MP) from the 173rd Airborne gives a suspect a drink near Vo Dat. (Army)

11

Troops from the 173rd Airborne at Vo Dat after a sweep two miles south of the town. The lead man carries a twelve gauge shotgun which was used in limited numbers by soldiers in the field. Most of the men carry extra rounds for the unit's M60 machine gun. (Army)

The Viet Cong were masters at camouflage and hiding. Troops searching a village try to flush out any VC in the tunnel and locate any other entrances by setting off a Red smoke grenade in the tunnel. All are equipped with M16 rifles and wear early pattern jungle fatigues. (Army)

A wounded guerrilla awaits medical help from soldiers of the 1st Cav near An Khe during late 1965. The VC and NVA were surprised by their treatment when captured by the Americans, unlike their treatment at the hands of the ARVN who were often cruel and vicious. (Army)

Marines search a hut during a ground sweep near Da Nang. Armed with M14 rifles, they have bloused their trouser legs to prevent leeches from crawling up their legs. (USMC)

A Marine M60 machine gun team watches as artillery fire falls on suspected VC positions during Operation HARVEST MOON, a large sweep in conjunction with ARVN troops south of Da Nang. Over 400 guerrillas were killed and large amounts of ammo, food and supplies were captured. (USMC)

Putting The Pressure On

The victories achieved during STARLIGHT, GIBRALTER and the Ia Drang Valley campaign did much to reverse the downward spiral of the early years of the Vietnam War. ARVN morale rose and American troops realized they could take on the NVA regulars and defeat them in battle. At the same time, however, GEN Westmoreland needed additional troops to engage the enemy and provide logistical support for the growing military presence in the embattled country. Eventually between 70-80 percent of American troop strength would be engaged in support activities and while only some twenty percent were in the field under fire, the brunt of the ground war was actually borne by only a small percentage of the U.S. forces in the country.

In early 1966, the 25th Infantry Brigade arrived and, teaming up with the 173rd Airborne and an Australian battalion, swept areas near the Cambodian border. They ran into little resistance, although large amounts of material were uncovered. In an earlier operation, the 173rd and the Aussies had decimated two VC battalions during seven days of operations near Cambodia, but the enemy now avoided combat, preferring instead to melt away into the jungle, underground bunkers or across the border into Cambodia. This was a common tactic of the VC and NVA when things became too rough inside Vietnam, since they knew that U.S. and ARVN forces were restricted from pursuing them into Cambodia.

This became a bone of contention between field commanders and headquarters in Saigon and Washington. On numerous occasions the border was violated, although rarely if ever was this reported. In some cases recon units, under secret orders from headquarters, moved inside Cambodia and Laos, under strict security. These "cross-border" operations were normally conducted by indigenous personnel under the supervision of a few Americans, usually Green Beret Special Forces troops, although later other units (Recon Marines and Navy SEALs) also took part in these missions.

Even though the communist troops avoided contact in the early months of 1966, allied units continued to expand their scope of operations. Suspected base camps were raided where large caches of arms, ammunition, equipment and documents were uncovered. Protection was also provided for the rice harvest but, while this helped some of the peasants, it also aided many absentee land owners in the cities who had been unable to get the rice while the VC controlled the area. This helped alienate the civilians, but unfortunately American officials were often totally unaware of the problem. This also played right into the VC's propaganda machine.

Following the Tet (a Vietnamese holiday similar to Christmas and New Year combined) truce, Operation MASHER/WHITE WING/THANG PHONG II began when units of the 1st Cavalry, ARVN and ROK Army started sweeps across Binh Dinh province to link up with Marines conducting Operation DOUBLE EAGLE. This combined operation was an attempt to destroy the 325th NVA Division. This was the first large scale operation carried out across corps boundaries and eventually netted close to 2,400 enemy dead by the time it ended in early March.

At this early stage of active U.S. involvement, the criteria used to declare victory was the "body count," since in this type of warfare little else of concrete value could be pointed to as an indication of success. While at first units tried to be fairly honest about enemy losses during engagements, pressure from higher command would eventually lead to distortions and padding of the numbers. Additionally, dead Vietnamese were usually counted as the enemy, although undoubtedly many innocent civilians died during actions between the two sides.

Unfortunately this desire to provide a tangible item with which to measure the war's progress provided little in the way of a true indication as to how the war was really going. Other things more subtle were a truer indication, but these were ignored because the "body count" was an easy and dramatic way to gauge progress and was easily understood in reports back in the U.S. In the end, this analysis would prove meaningless when other items were not factored into the overall war picture.

Contact in I Corps

In the early part of 1966, the North Vietnamese began to move units into I Corps from across the Demilitarized Zone (DMZ) which divided the two countries. Their goal was to inflict a substantial defeat on ARVN troops in the area and force American troops to be committed in order to save them. Hopefully this movement of U.S. troops would upset the pacification program and result in an increase in casualties, or perhaps even a victory for the NVA over the Marines. At first this move caused a great deal of concern in Saigon since the broken terrain, poor road network and lack of supply bases could seriously hamper American efforts in the area.

During early March the first in a series of clashes between allied forces and the NVA occurred. A joint Marine/ARVN task force encountered NVA troops in the vicinity of Quag Ngai city during Operation UTAH. In fierce fighting between 4 March and 8 March over 600 NVA were claimed as killed in exchange for 128 (98 Marines, 30 AVRN) Allied losses. Additionally, an unknown number of NVA were wounded compared to 278 Marines and 120 South Vietnamese. The fighting was some of the hardest of the war since the North Vietnamese were dug in and supported by machine guns, mortars and recoilless rifles. Heavy ground fire also damaged or destroyed a number of aircraft and helicopters flying in support of the Marines.

Further north, in Thua Thieu province, the 95th NVA regiment moved into the A Shau Valley and surrounded the Special Forces camp located in this natural infiltration route near the Laoian border. The camp, manned by a Civilian Irregular Defense Group (CIDG), was the only one left in the valley to monitor enemy movement. Two other camps, located at A Loui and Ta Bal, had been evacuated in December of 1965 leaving A Shau without any close fire support since it was beyond the range of allied artillery. Aerial resupply and support were available but heavy fog and cloud cover, the high mountains around the camp and concentrated anti-aircraft fire hindered this effort. The initial assault began in the early hours of 9 March with a heavy mortar barrage, followed up by a ground probe which pushed the defenders back to their main defense line.

The next day the NVA launched their final ground assault which began shortly after midnight. By late in the day the situation in camp was serious, despite air support, and plans were made to evacuate the remaining defenders. The evacuation lasted the better part of

Korean Marines load a 106MM recoilless rifle at their perimeter around Cam Ranh Bay. The gun crew are all equipped with M1 Garand rifles. As part of the agreement for sending troops to Vietnam, the South Koreans were to receive new equipment from the U.S. (Army)

To keep the VC as far away from their perimeter as possible, the Koreans carried out extensive patrols around Cam Ranh Bay. This patrol makes its way through a swamp several miles from the base. They carry both the old style World War Two "pineapple" grenade and the newer M26A1 fragmentation grenade. (Army)

The enemy was a master at infiltration, so whenever positions were set up for any length of time as much vegetation as possible was cleared away. These men from the 173rd use a scythe and lawnmower to clear away the underbrush. Lawnmowers were not normally used: troops usually used machetes, axes and other hand tools to do the job. (Army)

two days due to heavy ground fire and panic among the South Vietnamese. When the battle was finally over, allied losses included seven Green Berets, 250 CIDGs out of a garrison of 434 men, five aircraft shot down and over a dozen damaged. Some thought was given to moving two Marine battalions into the valley to recapture the camp and engage the NVA but due to a scarcity of reserves the plan was never put into effect and, for the time being, the valley was abandoned to the communists.

After A Shau, enemy activity around Quang Ngai picked up again. A joint drive, Operation TEXAS, ran into elements of three battalions from a VC and NVA regiment. Following TEXAS and Operation INDIANA, the focus of attention shifted to Chu Lai. Intelligence reports indicated that the 620th NVA division, with attached VC units, had moved into the area northwest of the Marine base. In an attempt to locate the enemy units, numerous recon teams were inserted into the area. The only significant contact occurred when an eighteen man team under SGT Jimmie Howard on Nui Vu hill was encircled and attacked on the night of 15/16 June. After holding out all night against an NVA battalion, a relief force was flown in which saved the twelve wounded survivors who were mostly armed with captured AK-47s. The members of the patrol received eighteen Purple Hearts, fifteen Silver Stars, two Navy Crosses and Howard himself received the Congressional Medal of Honor for his bravery and leadership.

Operation KANSAS never really expanded beyond the reconnaissance stages and lasted about one week, encountering little resistance. After its termination, recon teams stayed in the area, but aside from artillery and air strikes against suspected enemy troops concentrations, little contact was made. While no significant contact resulted, these Marine activities did help settle the area down, and their attention then shifted further north to the DMZ.

The DMZ

Enemy activity near the Demilitarized Zone (DMZ) which separated North and South Vietnam began during early 1966. Under GEN Westmoreland's direction the Marines conducted reconnaissance patrols around Khe Sanh near the Lao border, the site of an Army Special Forces camp. Eventually under his prodding, the Marines inserted a battalion onto the Khe Sanh plateau north of the camp, setting up an outpost and support base for the camp. It was hoped this move would locate any NVA forces in the area and forestall a situation like that which had occurred at A Shau. No contact resulted from Operation VIRGINIA and the Marines moved overland after its termination to check for enemy infiltration south of the DMZ along Route 9, again with no contact.

In Thua Thien province, the Marines, in conjunction with ARVN units, conducted numerous operations against NVA and VC units. Casualties, while not particularly heavy, could be high in single actions. Most actions, however, were relatively small, although to the grunts involved they were anything but insignificant.

By early summer, the major concern of both the Marines and Westmoreland had shifted further north to the DMZ. Intelligence reports indicated that the 324th NVA Division had moved into South Vietnam across the DMZ in violation of the agreements that stated military activity in the zone was prohibited. To counter this move, 8,500 Marines and 2,500 ARVN troops began operations in Quang Tri province bordering the DMZ in early July. Dubbed Operation HASTINGS, the offensive opened with a helicopter assault into the Nagan Valley on 15 July. The helicopters encountered heavy anti-aircraft fire, resulting in four helicopters being shot down. With a gallows sense of humor, the Marines nicknamed the area "Helicopter Valley."

This beginning was an indication of just how difficult HASTINGS was to be. For the next two weeks American and South Vietnamese forces slugged it out with the North Vietnamese. Heavy and accurate support fire from air and artillery units did much to help the allied troops in the rough terrain and thick jungles. Occasionally rain from an off-shore typhoon hindered air support and helicopter evacuation/resupply missions, but the NVA was slowly but methodically beaten down. By the end of July, when the operation was terminated, over 800 enemy soldiers were killed against 150 allied dead. The survivors of the 324th Division either withdrew into Laos or went into hiding in the dense jungles along the border to regroup.

Right after HASTINGS, another sweep, Operation PRAIRIE, was begun to determine if there were still sizeable NVA units located in the vicinity of the DMZ. Intelligence also indicated that two additional NVA divisions, the 304th and 341st, had moved into position just across the border within easy striking distance of allied positions and units. A recon team made first contact and precipitated a fierce fire fight with an NVA battalion. Following this, additional contacts were made by other companies inserted into the area from ground sweeps. Throughout August, the NVA displayed a willingness to stand and fight it out with the Marine units. Two Marine companies were surrounded by the NVA and despite air and artillery support were unable to break out until late in the operation.

As the fighting increased, more troops were airlifted into the region and an amphibious assault launched in support of the embattled Marines. PRAIRIE continued throughout the Fall and cost the Marines over 200 dead, but in return they killed more than 1,000 NVA regulars. Unfortunately, the communist presence in the area forced the Marines to divert troops from their pacification program, seriously hampering the program just as the Marine commanders had feared. In addition, the heavy casualties, due in part to attacking prepared positions, helped fuel the opponents of the war, although at this stage the anti-war movement was still in its infancy. Continued casualty figures like this, however, were a political asset for the communists who correctly figured that excessive casualties would erode home support for the war. As such, GEN Westmorland's strategy of attrition played right into their hands, which may or may not have been their real reason for initiating this and similar actions.

An M60 machine gun team from the 101st Airborne takes an enemy bunker under fire near Tuy Hoa on a search and destroy mission. The M60, although heavy, was an excellent weapon and provided heavy firepower for the troops in the field. (Army)

Though ARVN troops were used more and more for pacification, there were usually a number of battalions included during American ground sweeps. Each ARVN battalion had a U.S. advisor to help coordinate air or artillery support for it. An American advisor, armed with an M2 carbine, and his radio man move through a swamp south of Saigon. (Army)

15

An M60 machine gunner from the 1st Cav lays down fire as members of his unit take cover during Operation MASHER in Binh Binh Province. Both men carry extra ammunition belts for the M60. (Army)

An artillery team from the 173rd Airborne fire on enemy positions near Bien Hoa with a camouflage painted 105mm howitzer. (Army)

Operations Expand

American strength in Vietnam was growing daily and the tempo of action showed this increase across the whole country. Throughout early 1966, numerous operations were carried out wherever intelligence located suspected VC/NVA troop concentrations and base camps. Operation ROLLING STONE, carried out by the 1st Infantry Division, netted close to 200 enemy dead while the 101st's Operation HARRISON and the 25th Division's Operation GARFIELD captured large amounts of weapons, ammunition and supplies.

To support these and other operations required an ever growing logistical system and, as troop strength grew, so did the support units. Unfortunately, the ratio of combat troops to support troops was extremely poor, with five rear area troops being needed to support one combat trooper in the field. The vast array of material needed to keep the troops in the field supplied necessitated this ratio, seriously hampering the war effort since at any one time only a small portion of the total U.S. troops strength could be employed against the enemy. Although some of these troops were needed, there were serious questions raised about some of the things provided for the troops in the rear areas, since many of these "comfort" features never truly benefitted the "grunts" in the field, but throughout the war this situation was never adequately dealt with.

In order to capitalize on the successes gained on the battlefield, a major effort was begun to boast the Chieu Hoi or "open arms" program. This program was designed to entice individual guerrillas into voluntarily laying down their arms and siding with the South Vietnamese government. In return they received amnesty and financial aid to start over. Sometimes this was used by the VC when capture was imminent, but many guerrillas, tired of the fighting, disillusioned with the communist movement and realizing they had little chance of surviving, actually did embrace the program. Many of

these former VC later joined the South Vietnamese army or served with American units where they were known as "Kit Carson" Scouts. Most performed very well in this role and few deserted or returned to the communists.

As Summer approached, efforts were made to blunt an expected enemy offensive. In War Zone C, near Tay Vinh, elements of the 1st Infantry conducted a series of sweeps in an area where no ARVN troops had been for five years, uncovering and capturing large quantities of food, ammo and medical supplies. Further north, in the Central Highlands, the 101st and 25th Divisions conducted Operations HAWTHORNE and PAUL REVERE in conjunction with ARVN units around Kontum and Pleiku. Close to 1,100 VC and NVA were killed during these sweeps. Hard on the heels of their sweep through War Zone C, the 1st Infantry, along with the 5th ARVN Division, then moved north into Binh Long Province against the 9th VC Division in Operation EL PASO II. In this month long sweep, close to 900 VC were killed and the 9th was forced to scatter, many of the survivors retreating to Cambodia where they could rest and refit.

As the end of summer approached, additional troops arrived to augment allied strength. In late August elements of the 4th Infantry Division began to arrive in-country at Qui Nhon and, by the end of September, most of the division was in place in the Central Highlands around Pleiku. The 196th Infantry Brigade also came ashore in August and was assigned to Tay Ninh near War Zone C where it began to conduct operations almost immediately. In September, the 11th Armored Cavalry, the "Blackhorse Regiment," arrived for duty, the first armored unit to be specifically deployed for duty in Vietnam. Bringing with it tanks, APCs, self-propelled artillery and other mechanized equipment the unit was assigned to III Corps where the terrain was well suited for armor. The unit was initially employed for road clearance and security but soon began to team up with other units in ground sweeps and eventually would be used as the cutting edge in many sweeps through War Zone C and the Iron Triangle. The arrival of these units, along with additional support personnel, raised the total American strength to over 350,000 men, giving GEN Westmoreland enough troops to begin increasing the scope and magnitude of his ground operations.

The numerous waterways in Vietnam could be serious obstacles, so rafts were sometimes needed to cross them. Two members of the 173rd Airborne inflate a large raft which was brought in by a helicopter during a recon mission at the Dong Nai River. (Army)

Members of the 173rd Airborne use a raft to search for a suspected underwater Viet Cong bridge. On such missions the patrol had to be extra alert since an ambush under these conditions would be like shooting fish in the proverbial barrel. (Army)

Troops from the 9th ARVN Regiment board UH-1Ds of the 13th Aviation Battalion at Can Tho. Although the Vietnamese tried to build up their own helicopter assets, they still relied extensively on various American units to carry them into action. (Army)

Fall Operations

The newly arrived 196th Infantry Brigade wasted little time in getting into action. During the second week of September it began a sweep through War Zone C in Tay Ninh Province, code named Operation ATTLEBORO. Little contact was made during the initial stages but at the end of the first week, on 19 October, a sizeable VC/NVA base camp was discovered. From intelligence reports and captured documents, it was determined that the 9th VC Division, recently mauled by the 1st Infantry Division, had reentered South Vietnam from Cambodia. To reinforce the 196th, MACV ordered elements of the 1st Infantry, 4th Infantry, 173rd Airborne and a number of ARVN battalions into the area, making it the largest American operation to date.

By the end of the month contact had been made with several units of the Viet Cong division and fierce fighting broke out. It continued on into November and, by the end of the month, the 9th VC Division had again retreated into its sanctuaries in Cambodia (after losing over 1,000 men). The cost to the allies was not small: over 150 men being killed, with an additional 500 wounded. The most galling part of the entire operation, however, was the inability to pursue the enemy force into Cambodia. Just a few months before, the same VC unit had also retreated into Cambodia, safe in the knowledge that American troops could not pursue them. For both the men in the field and the top commanders this state of affairs was disheartening, but unfortunately the war was being run by civilian officials and politicians in Washington. This state of affairs would continue throughout the war and eventually lead to a tremendous cynicism on the part of the troops who risked their lives for questionable gains.

While ATTLEBORO was in progress, two other operations further north in Binh Dinh Province were also initiated. HAENG HO 6, a drive by the Korean Capital Division (Tigers) began on 23 September and ran until the first week in November. Its goal was to clear the area around Qui Nhon of VC units and their infrastructure. When completed on 9 November, over 1,100 VC lay dead for only light ROK casualties. North of Qui Nho, Operation IRVING was begun during the first week in October when units of the 1st Cav made a surprise helicopter assault against local VC forces at Hon Hoi who were ringed by ARVN and ROK units. Heavy fighting quickly developed but the VC were no match for the American troops and their firepower. After Hoa Hoi fell, the cavalrymen kept up pressure by making a series of airmobile assaults throughout the area over the next three weeks. When IRVING was terminated on 24 October, over 1,400 VC had either been killed or captured. This defeat devastated the communist hold on the area and pacification teams quickly moved in to reestablish government control. Due to their losses, the VC was unable to cause any serious hindrance and the area became relatively pacified for much of the remainder of the war.

Air support was vital to the troops on the ground and special teams of Air Force personnel were created to help direct air strikes. This Forward Air Controller (FAC) calls in a strike by F-100s against dug-in guerrillas north of Saigon. (USAF)

Other Air Force personnel were formed into Combat Control Teams (CCT) and were used to mark jump zones and direct aerial resupply missions. This five man team watches as ARVN paratroopers drop into a DLZ they have just marked north of Saigon during a sweep of suspected VC Camps. (USAF)

The large number of air bases in South Vietnam required a great deal of security since the bases made lucrative targets for the guerrillas. An Air Police Sergeant monitors the flight line at Da Nang to keep unauthorized vehicles and personnel away from the F-4 Phantoms in the background. (USAF)

Night was the prime time for infiltration, and for the security men on duty around the airfield perimeter, every sound could be a potential enemy sapper. The monsoon rains often made their job more difficult since it could cover the movement of enemy troops. (USAF)

As 1966 drew to a close, there was little slackening in the war effort. Near the Cambodian border around Pleiku the newly arrived 4th Infantry Division conducted Operation PAUL REVERE IV from mid-October until the end of the year. Supported by elements of the 1st Cav and 25th Infantry Division, the 4th made daily sweeps in the region and maintained almost continuous contact with the NVA and VC. Heavy fighting often developed, but with the border so close the communists were able to retreat into Cambodia when things became too hot for them. The operation cost the enemy close to 1,000 dead, but the 4th did not find this victory easy, losing a considerable number of men during the two and a half month campaign. In one instance the division was hit by a mortar barrage of over 500 shells as the NVA began to bring more crew served weapons into play due to their proximity to the border.

Along the coast in Binh Dinh Province the 1st Cav began Operation THAYER II on 25 October, right after the termination of Operation IRVING and THAYER I. It swept the rich, fertile coastal plains along the coast and then moved westward into the Luoe Ci and Kim Son valleys, major guerrilla strongholds. Large amounts of weapons and supplies were uncovered and over 1,700 Viet Cong were killed. The operation ran into 1967 and was finally terminated in mid-February. Further south, around Saigon, a multi-battalion sweep around the capital was conducted by a one battalion from the 1st, 4th, and 25th Infantry Divisions under the code name Operation FAIRFAX (on 30 November). In January of 1967 these units returned to their parent divisions and the operation was continued by the 199th Infantry Brigade, who later, in turn, handed over control of it to the 5th ARVN Ranger Group.

In mid-December additional reinforcements arrived in-country to augment American strength. The 9th Infantry Division, which had been specifically reactivated for service in Vietnam, was assigned to III Corps, with its headquarters at Bear Cat, southeast of Saigon. The division raised the total level of U.S. strength in Vietnam to 385,000 men. The division's 2nd Brigade was assigned to work with the Mobile Riverine Force (MRF), the first time since the Civil War that the Army had employed troops from floating bases. It was also the first major American combat formation to deploy to the Delta region, which had been under the sole responsibility of the ARVN.

As the year closed out, the overall situation had taken on a decidedly positive outlook for the U.S. and its allies. Troops strength had risen dramatically and in numerous operations the North Vietnamese and Viet Cong had been dealt decisive defeats. These victories had raised South Vietnamese morale and had helped the pacification program by driving the guerrillas away from many populated regions. The influx of ground troops had ensured that the communists could not achieve a military victory and their only safe havens were "sanctuaries" in Laos and Cambodia. Aside from this, GEN Westmoreland and the MACV high command were pleased with the progress of the war and anticipated even better results in the upcoming year.

Air Force FAC pilots also lived in the field on forward airfields. These O-1 Bird Dog spotter pilots often flew out of forward landing strips or even rough LZs if the need arose. This O-1 shares a forward strip with Army UH-1 and OH-13 helicopters. (USAF)

This VNAF C-47 was destroyed by a VC mortar attack during the night. Mortars and rockets were particularly feared since there was little defense against them and most people had little indication there was anything wrong until the rounds began to fall. (USAF)

Although the 1st Cav was noted for its helicopter assaults, it did have a ground element. Troops of the 1st Cav move out to the forward support area during Operation MASHER, a major multi-unit sweep in Binh Dinh Province by American and ARVN units. (Army)

A member of the 1st Cav scans the terrain in front of him for signs of the enemy during Operation MASHER. He has used an old Green towel to help break up the outline of his helmet and carries an M72 LAW (Light Anti-tank Weapon), a disposal 66MM one shot rocket launcher used against bunkers and armor. (Army)

As part of the operation, the Marines crossed over into the providence with their DOUBLE EAGLE ground sweep. This Air Force HH-3 brings in a 105MM howitzer for a Marine artillery unit during the operation. (USMC)

(Above) Members of the 1st Cav return to the la Drang Valley during Operation LINCOLN in the Spring of 1966, but little of the fierce fighting from the Fall battle occurred. The RTO in front has folded his antenna down to make him less conspicuous. RTOs were often prime targets for snipers during the initial stages of a firefight. (Army)

(Above - Right) When enemy bunkers were discovered during a sweep, efforts were made to render them useless to the enemy after they had been searched. These soldiers of the 101st Airborne prepare to blow a bunker during Operation VAN BUREN, a joint US/Korean/ARVN sweep in Phu Yen Province. (Army)

(Right) A squad leader points out a suspected enemy position to his company commander during Operation BOX SPRING in March of 1966. All three wear flak vests to provide protection against shrapnel and small arms fire. The radio telephone operator (RTO - right) carries several smoke grenades for marking either friendly or enemy positions. (Army)

(Below) Enemy activity in the northern provinces kept the Marines constantly on sweeps to forestall any communist buildup. These Marines depart from an LZ as a H-34 lifts off behind them. The helicopter door gunner remains alert for any possible enemy activity. (USMC)

A new weapon was introduced into the war during the Spring of 1966, the Patrol Air Cushion Vehicle (PACV), which floated atop a giant air pocket. During its initial use by the Navy it patrolled the coastline to cut down on seaborne infiltration. The crew of this PACV check the papers of this junk to be sure all is in order. (Navy)

Heat was a constant enemy to both friend and foe alike and most troops carried as much water as possible unless they knew they would be near a water supply. A squad leader from the 1st Infantry Division takes a long drink from a two-quart collapsible canteen during a clearing operation in Long Khanh Providence, east of Saigon. (Army)

Later PACVs were tried out on the Plain of Reeds north of the Mekong Delta. This was a swampy area bordering on Cambodia. This PACV has surprised a sampan which was carrying a VC who tried to hide underwater by breathing through a reed. Unfortunately for him the crew of the PACV spotted and captured him. (Navy)

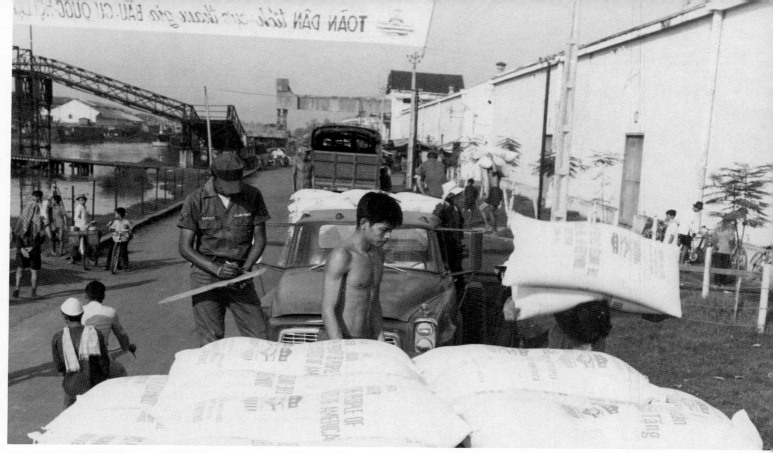

A great deal of food and material was sent to Vietnam to help the people. Supposedly distributed free, corrupt officials often sold it on the Black market for an immense profit and American soldiers found it on numerous occasions in V.C. supply dumps. This food is being loaded onto trucks for shipment to remote hamlets, but chances are it will not reach them. (USAF)

In an effort to detect the enemy, scout dogs were brought in-country to work with selected units. Results were mixed with the dogs proving effective around bases in security roles but less effective in the field where the heat often sapped their strength. One set of dogs given to the ARVN were eaten by the troops within a few days as dog was considered a delicacy by the Vietnamese. (Army)

War can be hell but these men from the 101st Airborne seem to be enjoying themselves as they ride on captured "VC" ponies during Operation JOHN PAUL JONES near Tuy Hoa. (Army)

A Marine M48A3 Patton tank moves through a corn field during Operation MACON, in Quang Nam Providence near An Hoa. Though restitution was supposed to be paid to the farmer whose crops were destroyed during such sweeps, often the money went into the hands of corrupt officials which alienated the local people and made them more sympathetic to the enemy. (USMC)

During field operations Fire Support Bases were set up to provide artillery support for troops in the field. Besides their artillery, these bases usually had an infantry company for base defense since these positions were inviting targets to the enemy. Troops of the 1st Cav construct bunkers for defense of such a base after a large area has been cleared to provide for wide fields of fire. (Army)

While the war was being waged in the field, pacification moved ahead at good speed and this officer found some new friends in a village near Saigon. Unfortunately, high officials failed to realize the importance of pacification and worried more about high body counts as a way to show how well the war was progressing. (Army)

The newly arrived 11th ACR was quickly committed to action despite fears that tanks would have little use in Vietnam. The "Black Horse" Regiment showed just how effective armor could be in this type of warfare. These M48A3s have deployed in a "herringbone" formation to cover both sides of the road during a possible ambush. Every other vehicle pivoted outward at the first sign of danger. (Army)

M113 Armored Personnel Carriers (APCs) of the 25th Infantry Division, B Troop, 3 Squadron, 4th Cavalry move forward during Operation CEDAR FALLS conducted in January of 1967.

An Air Force Combat Control team directs a paradrop during Operation JUNCTION CITY in February of 1967. Both men are dressed in Tiger stripe fatigues and Black berets.

A soldier of the 25th Infantry Division moves across a small stream near Duc Pho during a sweep of Highway 1 in the Summer of 1967.

American and ARVN Special Forces troops question locals about the whereabouts of VC guerrillas in the Central Highlands. The Vietnamese are dressed in camouflaged fatigues called "Tiger Stripes." (Army)

The single greatest danger to armored vehicles were mines which could either stop them, making them easy targets, or totally destroy them. These troops check for mines during a road mission near Long Giai. (Army)

Efforts were made to increase the ability of small villages to protect themselves during this time. A member of the Civilian Irregular Defense Group (CIDG) takes part in a training exercise outside his village. He is armed with a twelve gauge shotgun, a good weapon for close in fighting. (Army)

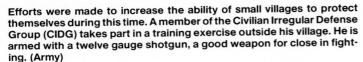

Air Force controllers direct a C-123 into Dau Tieng during Operation ATTLEBORO. This operation was the largest U.S. ground operation up to this time and resulted in close to 1,200 enemy dead. (USAF)

An Army C-7 Caribou lifts off from a remote strip during Operation ATTLEBORO, a major sweep into War Zone C during the Fall of 1966. The Caribou was later involved in a clash between the Army and Air Force. The Air Force felt that they should possess transport aircraft and eventually the Army lost the battle. (USAF via Bell)

M113 Armored Personnel Carriers (APCs) from the 11th Armored Cavalry Regiment take part in Operation ALEXANDRIA near Xuan Loc. When fitted with various shields and both .50 caliber and M60 machine guns, the M113s were called ACAVs, short for Armored Cavalry Assault Vehicles. (Army)

Armored units required extensive support to keep them supplied in the field. These ACAVs of the 11th ACR take on fuel and ammunition from a supply column during a sweep north of Saigon. Resupply convoys were prime targets for the enemy and had to be heavily guarded to insure that they got through to their intended units. (Army)

Troops take cover after coming under sniper fire while on operations in War Zone C. The infantryman in the foreground is armed with an XM-148, an M16 rifle fitted with a 40mm grenade launcher. (Army)

Using a rope ladder, troops descend from a hovering CH-47 into War Zone C during Operation JUNCTION CITY. This method was used when there was no suitable Landing Zone (LZ) for the helicopter to land. (Army)

These soldiers take advantage of a stream to wash. In field operations troops might go for weeks before being able to return to base camp and they took advantage of every chance to get clean. (Army)

Marines man an anti-mortar radar unit on a beach near the DMZ. The M48 in the background had the dual role of security and counter-battery fire against any VC/NVA mortar attacks. (USMC)

An officer from the 1st Infantry Division, Big Red One, calls in artillery fire during Operation ATTLEBORO in War Zone C. The ability to quickly communicate with supporting arms was a vital part of any operation. (Army)

A squad of Marines sweep a road for mines while being covered by a Marine M48 Patton tank. The dense jungle made infantry support for the tanks an absolute must. (USMC)

War is often boring and any action is sometimes preferable to just sitting around. These men from the 101st Airborne wait for a ride during Operation PICKETT near Kontum in the Central Highlands. When carrying ammo like this the gunner had to be sure that the rounds were clean or they could jam the M60. (Army)

On the Offensive

With the NVA and VC on the defensive due to the serious losses suffered at the hands of U.S. troops, GEN Westmoreland decided to seize the initiative and strike out at enemy positions northwest of Saigon. Targeted for this attack were two long time VC sanctuaries, the Iron Triangle and War Zone C. The Iron Triangle was an area between War Zones C and D in a trackless, thick jungle area crisscrossed by hundreds of miles of tunnels and bunker complexes. Filled with ammunition, supplies and support facilities, this area served as a staging and rest area for VC troops carrying out attacks in the Saigon area. Well defended, ARVN forces had rarely entered the zone and then in only large numbers for short periods of time. A combined American, Australian, New Zealand and ARVN attack had tried to crack the jungle redoubt during late 1965 but had met with little success and after their departure the enemy rebuilt what had been destroyed.

To destroy the Iron Triangle once and for all, GEN Westmoreland launched Operation CEDAR FALLS on 8 January 1967. The first part of the attack began with an airmobile assault on the village of Ben Suc. Close on the heels of this came a series of thrusts by ground units to isolate and destroy enemy forces. From the west, elements of the 25th Infantry Division and 196th Infantry Brigade moved into blocking positions, while from the east and north units of the 1st Infantry Division, the 173rd Airborne Brigade and the 11th Armored Cavalry Regiment (ACR) set up their positions. The next day units from these maneuver elements began to crisscross the area in search of an estimated two regiments of VC. Unfortunately, the enemy had been forewarned and managed to either slip away or hide in the labyrinth of tunnels in the area and contacts were few.

For three weeks the troops searched the entire area but to little avail. Although over 700 enemy troops were killed this was small compared to the numbers of troops employed in the sweep and the enemy troop strength in the area. American losses were 72 dead, relatively light, but overall CEDAR FALLS achieved relatively little when compared to the effort put into it. Even efforts to destroy the numerous tunnels and bunker complexes within the Triangle were only partially successful and when the troops withdrew from the area, the VC began to move back in and rebuild their bases.

Within a month of the termination of CEDAR FALLS another massive offensive, the largest to date by American forces, was launched against War Zone C by twenty-two American and four ARVN battalions. Dubbed Operation JUNCTION CITY, this operation ran nearly three months and was divided into three phases. The first part

The Australian and New Zealand contingent were reinforced during 1966 and joined together as a Task Force with their own supporting arms. This column of Australian M113s takes part in Operation INGHRAM southeast of Saigon toward the end of 1966. (Army)

began on 22 February when the various units moved into place to surround the war zone which ran north and west from the area around Ben Cat to the Cambodian border. In the east and north elements from the 1st and 9th Infantry Division, the 173rd Airborne Brigade the 1st Cavalry Regiment and ARVN units took up blocking positions. In the northwestern and western sectors, units from the 25th and 4th Infantry Division, the 196th Light Infantry Brigade, the 11th ACR and Vietnamese Marines moved in to close off avenues of escape in this direction. From the south other elements from the 25th Infantry and the 11th ACR would push into the "horseshoe" shaped perimeter created by the these units. A unique aspect of the first phase was the first (and only) large scale parachute drop by American forces of the war. This occurred on the first day when the 173rd Airborne dropped near the village of Katum in the eastern sector in order to free up helicopter assets for other units involved in the operation.

During this initial phase the VC tried to avoid the various elements sweeping the area. Only twice was there large scale fighting, both times near the village of Prek Klok. In the first battle, the enemy attacked a company from the 1st Infantry Division while in the second, guerrillas tried to overrun a fire support base. In both cases the American troops were able to hold out and inflict heavy casualties on the VC while suffering relatively low losses themselves.

In the second phase, the fighting picked up as the enemy lost room to maneuver in the shrinking perimeter. From mid-March, when phase two began, there was almost daily contact. The VC, desperate to escape, hit fire support bases, units in the field, defending fixed positions and LZs with a vengeance. Fierce fighting, sometimes hand-to-hand, took place at Suoi Tre, Ap Bau Bang, and Ap Gu, in addition to a number of smaller actions during daily sweeps. On occasions only the timely arrival of reinforcements saved American forces and the enemy was never able to inflict a serious defeat on U.S. troops.

By mid-April, the final phase of the operation was put into effect. Decimated by heavy losses, the few VC troops left in the ever shrinking perimeter were unable to effectively resist the allied forces and were run to ground as the various American units closed in on the few unswept areas. The operation was officially terminated on 14 May due to a lack of contact and the need to redeploy units to other critical areas. In the final analysis JUNCTION CITY was far more successful then CEDAR FALLS in both enemy casualties and material damage. Over 2,700 VC were killed, tons of supplies and documents were captured and close to one hundred base camps were destroyed. The cost was not cheap, with 282 American servicemen killed in the three month operation, along with the numerous wounded and material destroyed or damaged. More importantly, however, the operation showed the enemy that no area within South Vietnam was safe from attack, forcing the communists to rethink their strategy and restructure their logistics system.

A specially constructed raft built by Army engineers moves along the Saigon River to catch guerrillas who are trying to escape from troops engaged in Operation NIAGARA FALLS. A power boat provides propulsion and the craft is armed with a "Quad 50" four gun .50 caliber anti-aircraft mount and several M60s. (Army)

Operation CEDAR FALLS was an attempt to destroy the enemy bastions in the Iron Triangle. A soldier from the 1st Infantry Division takes cover behind gravestones at Ben Suc as he watches for signs of enemy action in the village. (Army)

A column of M113s and M48s from the 1st Infantry Division move along a road through a rubber plantation during Operation CEDAR FALLS. The well maintained lines of rubber trees provided the enemy with wide lanes of fire and armor proved to be highly useful under these conditions. (Army)

Troops of the 1st Infantry Division ride on an M48A3 of the 4th Cavalry Regiment during Operation JUNCTION CITY.

An M42A1 Duster of Battery C, 1st Battalion, 44th Artillery supports Marines engaging VC and NVA troops near Dong Ha.

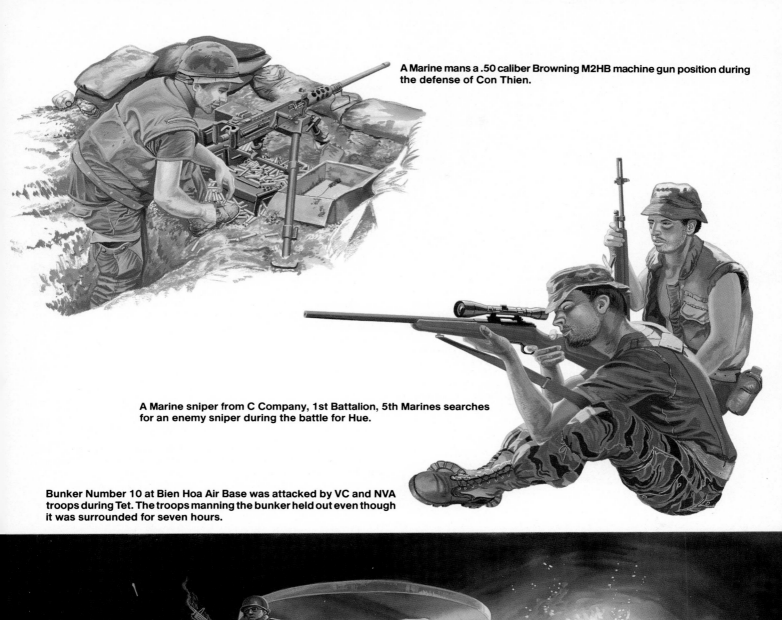

A Marine mans a .50 caliber Browning M2HB machine gun position during the defense of Con Thien.

A Marine sniper from C Company, 1st Battalion, 5th Marines searches for an enemy sniper during the battle for Hue.

Bunker Number 10 at Bien Hoa Air Base was attacked by VC and NVA troops during Tet. The troops manning the bunker held out even though it was surrounded for seven hours.

A machine gunner from the 25th Infantry Division takes a sniper under fire during Operation CEDAR FALLS near Cu Chi. He has draped a cloth from his helmet over the back of his neck to provide some protection from the hot sun. (Army)

Hard on the heels of CEDAR FALLS came Operation JUNCTION CITY, a major drive into War Zone C. The only combat jump of the war by an Army Airborne unit occurred during this drive. The 173rd Airborne made this jump to free helicopter assets for other uses. An artillery unit of the brigade receives a resupply drop from an Air Force C-130. (Army)

The new Army CH-47 Chinook heavy lift helicopter proved invaluable in ferrying in men and material to troops during the operation. A jeep and trailer are unloaded in a clearing during the initial stages of the sweep. (Army via Bell)

Air Force tactical air control teams played an important part in the resupply effort. These airmen watch supplies, which were air dropped under their direction, land at a forward base. (USAF)

Seizing the Initiative

Following Operation CEDAR FALLS and JUNCTION CITY, American forces began a series of concerted drives throughout the country to destroy or drive out all major NVA and VC units. Throughout the Spring and Summer of 1967, additional manpower came in to increase American and allied troop strength, permitting GEN Westmoreland to move units as the need arose. In particular, the 1st Cav became something of a mobile reserve, being shifted around as the situation warranted. Allied units also played an increasingly important part in the overall ground effort. Along the central coastal region elements of two South Korean divisions conducted numerous ground sweeps which resulted in nearly 900 enemy dead and did much to pacify the region. Further south, the Australian and New Zealand contingents, working in conjunction with American and ARVN forces swept around the Saigon region in an attempt to clear out long time guerrilla strongholds.

In the Delta region a new type of American unit was created for employment among the numerous waterways and canals in this vital agricultural region. This unit was the Mobile Riverine Force (MRF) which combined elements of the 9th Infantry Division with a Navy task force made up of modified landing craft. The "Brown Water Navy" provided transportation, escort and fire support for the troops as they conducted a series of mini-amphibious assaults in the Delta region. Although the Marines would have been better suited for such operations and had carried out such attacks earlier in the region, they were heavily committed in I Corps and couldn't be redeployed to the area.

In the northern portions of I Corps the Marines did indeed face serious problems from the North Vietnamese. Able to strike from across the DMZ and Laos, the NVA kept up constant pressure on Marine positions. To counter this the Marines carried out numerous air assaults and ground sweeps to keep the communists off balance. While some resulted in little contact, others such as Operations PRAIRIE II, UNION I/II, DESOTO and SWIFT led to heavy fighting and severe losses for the NVA. Due to the severity of the situation, more Army troops were redeployed into the area, allowing the Marines to concentrate most of their strength in the northern part of the corps area and near the DMZ. Aside from the need to reinforce the area, there was also a desire by Washington, Saigon and MACV to build a series of fortified positions along the DMZ to provide defense against a push by the NVA and allow for better observation.

Though the Marines were basically opposed to such a set up, they were forced to follow orders and work began on a series of fortified position just south of the zone. One base, Con Thieu, was singled out for special attention by the North Vietnamese and in the early Summer of 1967, the NVA began raining artillery fire down on the Marines from the DMZ and moved troops into the region. To counter this, Operation BUFFALO was launched in early July to relieve pressure on Con Thieu. Supported by air, armor and artillery the Marines made a series of sweeps which decimated the 90th NVA regiment and threw back this new enemy offensive. More fighting was to come, but numerous lessons had been learned in this first major encounter in which the enemy was supported by heavy, sustained artillery support.

Troops riding on top of an M113 from the 9th Infantry Division provide security during a medical civic action program (MED-CAP) at the village of Ap Tinh Thi. Troops were discouraged from riding with their legs over the sides of the vehicle since if it hit a mine the explosion might take off a leg. (Army)

The Viet Cong were masters at hiding arms and equipment, making a careful search necessary when troops swept through a village. A trooper from the 1st Cav carefully looks into the thatched roof of a hut to see if any supplies are hidden there. The searcher had to be careful of possible booby traps, anything from explosives to a poisonous snake. (Army)

A guard bunker outside the entrance to a small Army compound. Sandbag bunkers had to be rebuilt from time to time as the sandbags deteriorated in the tropical conditions and simply fell apart. (Author)

Troops of the Mobile Riverine Force take a break in the mud during operations in the Mekong Delta. Both men carry extra ammunition belts for the unit's M60 machine gun. (Army)

Troops gather around a jeep armed with a .50 caliber Browning M2HB machine gun on the passenger side. The driver has a piece of armor positioned in front of him as a small bit of added protection. (Bob Krenkel)

An M102 155mm Howitzer of A Battery, 2/19 Artillery at LZ Geronimo north of Bong Son during December of 1967. The muzzle blast of this gun was severe and ruptured eardrums were common among crew members. (Glenn Sheathelm)

Troops of the 47th Infantry ford a stream in the Mekong Delta. Operations conducted in the delta were limited to less than a week so that the troops could dry out and avoid problems such as immersion foot. (Army)

Training in the use of morters, Vietnamese Regional Forces fill sandbags as they build a mortar pit for their 4.2 inch mortar. Each heavy mortar platoon was equipped with four mortar tubes. (Bob Krenkel)

Vietnamese Regional Forces inspect a 4.2 inch mortar. The 4.2 mortar was the largest mortar in Army service and has a maximum range of 5,650 meters. (Bob Krenkel)

A CH-47 Chinook lifts off after bringing in a load of supplies to a fire support base. The aircraft is armed with a .50 caliber machine gun in the crew door. (Bob Krenkel)

The Border Battles

Throughout the Summer and Fall of 1967, American and allied troops kept up the pressure on the NVA and VC. Aside from the NVA threat in I Corps, the enemy seemed to draw back, stung by the series of defeats inflicted on him by the hard charging U.S. troops. For the time being, the communists began to revert to their old strategy of ambushes, booby traps, sapper attacks and sniping. Rarely would the enemy stand and fight and then only when it was on favorable terms for them. As the various ground sweeps pushed the NVA and VC units back toward the border, they were able to draw on their supplies and replacements, which enabled them to rebuild many shattered formations.

Starting in the Fall of 1967, the enemy began making attacks along the border areas of Laos and Cambodia. These attacks, however, seemed to lack any overall objective. The first phase of these seemingly random battles occurred around Song Be in Phuoc Long Province where an ARVN battalion held out against an NVA regiment. At the end of October another NVA regiment attempted to overrun the town of Loc Ninh, defended only by local troops, but were also repulsed with heavy casualties. Reacting quickly, elements of the 1st Infantry Division moved into the area and came under heavy fire in the plantations which surrounded the town. Only with aid of heavy firepower were the U.S. troops able to force the enemy out of their prepared positions, which had excellent fields of fire in the cultivated rows of trees. While over 1,000 enemy troops died, American casualties were over 200 killed and wounded.

Further north, the enemy began to move troops into the area around Dak To, near the juncture point of Vietnam, Cambodian and Laos. Aside from having a small special Forces camp, Dak To was important because it overlooked Route 512 which served as a major enemy infiltration avenue into the Central Highlands and Route 14 which was the main north-south road in the area.

By late October enough intelligence information had been compiled to show that the 1st NVA Division (Reinforced) had moved into the area around the town. To counter this move, units of the 4th Infantry Division were airlifted into the area to carry out Operation MACARTHUR. Evidence soon surfaced which indicated that the enemy would use three regiments to attack the town while the fourth was kept in reserve to either exploit any victories or cover a retreat. Additional elements from the 4th, along with a battalion of the 173rd Airborne Brigade, were rushed in as reinforcements and began to sweep the region.

Almost immediately heavy fighting erupted between the dug in NVA and the U.S. troops. Artillery and air strikes, including B-52 missions, were needed to help the infantry drive the enemy troops out of their well concealed and heavily fortified positions. By mid-November the Americans had managed to gain the upper hand and the NVA commander began a methodical retreat to the safety of Cambodia and Laos. To cover this retreat, he emplaced his reserve regiment on Hill 875 (named for its height above sea level) in order to tie up the American forces which had to be helicoptered into the area. In this way he hoped to divert attenion away from the three retreating regiments.

A patrol from the 173rd soon discovered the dug in NVA troops and a battalion size assault was quickly mounted. Despite heavy support fire, the battalion could make little headway up the steep, rugged slope against the well fortified enemy troops. Pinned down by intense fire, another battalion was brought in to help its sister unit take the hill. Fighting raged for four days and another battalion from the 4th was brought in to help out the two from the 173rd. This finally tipped the balance and on Thanksgiving Day the tired U.S. troops stormed over to the top of Hill 875. This marked the end, effectively, of the fighting around Dak To specifically and the border battles in general.

Although at the time the enemy's objectives for this Fall campaign were questioned, in retrospect American officers later felt the NVA High Command used these battles as a means to divert American attention away from preparations for the Tet Offensive, pull U.S. troops away from population centers and inflict serious casualties on American forces to help fuel the growing anti-war sentiment in the U.S. For in the fighting around Dak To and Hill 875 alone, over 300 U.S. troops were killed and even though the NVA lost over 1,600, the news media quickly homed in on these casualty figures which played right into the enemy's hands. Thus, despite their battlefield setbacks, the communists had laid the ground work for their political strategy which would bear fruit within the next six months.

Action in the northern provinces continued to pick up as the Marines kept up pressure on the VC and NVA. These Marines take cover behind a paddy dike as they draw fire from the treeline (right) along CR 1, the infamous "Street Without Joy." The Marines are armed with M14s since the M16 was still viewed with skepticism due to its light-weight construction. (USMC)

Much has been written about the American atrocities at My Lai, yet the press focused little on the savage behavior of the VC and NVA. These three teenage girls, members of a Revolutionary Development Team, were murdered in cold blood by the VC after being captured in the hamlet of Suoi Chan. All three have their hands tied behind their backs and have been shot through the back of the head. (Army)

Terror was sometimes random and innocent civilians suffered the consequences. These people were on a bus which hit a mine near Phu My. Three small children, four women and two men were killed in the blast while eleven others were wounded. Yet little was heard in the American press about incidents like this. (Army)

Getting supplies to troops in the field could often be a problem. In the hilly regions up north there was little room for helicopters to land but Marine pilots came up with ways to overcome this. While this CH-46 hovers with its tail door down against the hill side, Marines quickly unload rations. Such flying took great skill, concentration and team-work among the crew. (USMC)

M113 ACAVs set up a blocking position near Tan Son Nhut Air Base to prevent VC units from escaping down the road. Every other vehicle is facing a different direction to cover each other. (Terry Love)

155MM howitzers of K Battery, 12th Marine Regiment, 2nd Marine Division fire on NVA positions in support of an Army operation near Quang Ngai in 1967. (James Holler)

M48A-3s and M113 ACAVs along the road at Tan Son Nhut Air Base. These armored units were given the task of routing out die hard VC units that had gained access to the base. (Terry Love)

An M113 ACAV of the 11th ACR waits on the outskirts of Saigon for orders to move into the city. The M113 ACAV was a modification of the basic M113 APC with extra guns and gun shields. (Terry Love)

Marines take cover during Operation NEW CASTLE as they receive fire from entrenched Viet Cong troops. The vehicle behind them is an LVTE-5A1, an engineering version of the basic amtrac personnel carrier. The plow on the front was used to dig up mines on occasion and was nicknamed the "Potato Digger." (USMC)

An officer and his RTO dash forward as a Marine rifleman covers them with his M14. Officers and RTOs were prime targets in the opening minutes of a battle as the enemy knew that the RTO was usually the only way the troops could call in support fire. If both he and the officer could be hit, the enemy might be able to escape with few losses. (USMC)

This Marine prepares to fire an M72 LAW against a cement gate off to the right. Although a useful weapon, the LAW had a tendency to misfire if carried too long, because of moisture. The Marine also carries a pair of heavy duty civilian type gloves in his belt, probably to protect his hands from the thick thorny vegetation in the area. (USMC)

The shortage of helicopters to support ARVN units often meant that there had to be an airdrop of troops on an ARVN operation. These troops from the 67th Airborne Division float down on their drop zone from USAF C-130 transports during an operation in the Mekong Delta. The smoke marks both the DZ and shows how the wind is blowing. (Army)

Troops from the 1st Cav receive a hot meal during Operation PERSHING in the An Lao Valley. Although appreciated, the sudden change in food from their normal field rations sometimes caused digestive and personal sanitation problems for the troops. (Army)

Members of the 25th Infantry Division take a break while on convoy duty near Cu Chi during Operation ROUTE BLUE. Each man carries a wide variety of personal gear and no two men look alike with respect to what and how they carried their equipment. (Army)

To aide in bunker busting, the Marines used the 106MM recoilless rifle mounted a number of different ways. This weapon is mounted on an M274 Mechanical Mule, a lightweight vehicle designed for air transport. The flat trajectory of the 106 made it an ideal weapon for hitting small targets. (USMC)

A barge mounted 105MM howitzer of the 3rd Battalion, 34th Artillery, 9th Infantry Division fire on VC/NVA positions in support of a sweep in the Mekong Delta. Army troops operated in conjunction with the sailors of the "Brown Water Navy" who supplied support for the floating gun batteries. (Army)

Carrying M60 ammunition belts, two grunts from the 35th Infantry Regiment, 25th Division moved through dense jungle near Duc Pho. The jungle climate was hard on the tropical uniforms, but resupply was often spotty and troops sometimes went for weeks at a time with uniforms torn and worn like this. (Army)

An M79 Grenadier relaxes in the shade of a captured umbrella while on a sweep around Due Pho during June of 1967. The M79 fired a 40MM shell accurately over a range of 400 meters and could fire a number of different types of shells. (Army)

The 106MM recoilless rifle was man-portable, being carried by four men (over a short distance). This 106 from the 1st Cav was being used to destroy a bunker near An Khe during the Spring of 1967. Its large back blast, however, made it easy to spot, limiting its use. (Army)

An RTO and his company commander take cover as an air strike hits a guerrilla position in a tree line. The rapid response by air and artillery fire was invaluable in a war where a few minutes could make a great deal of difference. (Army)

A squad from the 1st Cav hastily set up a defense position along the outer edges of their LZ during Operation MASHER conducted in Quang Nhai Province. Often the enemy would let the lead elements come in to the LZ before opening fire, trapping a relatively small force in an attempt to score a quick victory. (Army)

A Marine cleans his M16 during a sweep south of Dia Loc. Following problems with jamming during fighting around Khe Sanh, the chamber assembly was replaced by one with a chrome plating. This greatly helped to solve the jamming problem although the weapon needed to be cleaned as often as possible. (USMC)

Mines were a constant problem for men, tanks and APCs. The VC used both ones brought in from other communist states and a variety of homemade ones, such as this one constructed from a tin can and a twenty-five pound charge of plastic explosive. The VC in particular were experts at fashioning mines out of discarded American junk and American troops made little effort to destroy such material, providing the enemy with a valuable source of material. (Army)

An M109 self-propelled howitzer from the 11th ACR provides artillery support during Operation AKRON. The machine gun shield is a Vietnam modification, added to protect the vehicle commander from the ever present danger of sniper fire. (Army)

A "Chue Hoi" interrogates a captured Viet Cong during PHU DONG 24, an ARVN operation conducted in Vinh Long Province, southwest of Saigon. Often ARVN troops were incredibly brutal in their treatment of prisoners, although no more than the communists. (Army)

Elements of the 4th Infantry Division conducted Operation FRANCIS MARION west of Pleku for nearly half of 1967, killing over 1,200 NVA and VC. Troops await their marker smoke to clear from an LZ midway through the sweep. It was often necessary for the men to clear away trees so that the helicopters could pick them up. (Army)

Mines, while unable to destroy a tank, could blow off a tread and immobilize the vehicle. This M48A3 was disabled by just such a mine, a common occurrence during the war. (Army)

Troops from the 9th Infantry Division were carried into action by modified landing craft called Armored Troop Carriers (ATCs). Fire support was provided by Monitors (modified landing craft fitted with a 40MM cannon and other weapons). Some ATCs were fitted with a small helicopter landing platform. The MRF did much to hinder the VC in the Delta, regaining much lost territory. (Navy)

American troops had not been committed to the Mekong Delta for a number of reasons early in the war, but that changed in 1967 when the Mobile Riverine Force (MRF) was created to fight in the Delta. Based on barracks ships such as the USS BENEWAH (APA-35), the troops were deployed as needed. (Navy)

A UH-1D comes in for a landing on a modified ATC. Some ATCs were fitted out with hospital facilities and UH-1 Medivacs were able to save many lives by the quick transfer of wounded to these floating aid stations. (Navy)

Additional support for the MRF and its troops was provided by the Assault Support Patrol Boats (ASPBs), designed specifically for use in Vietnam. Armed with 20mm cannons, machine guns and grenade launchers, these vessels swept for mines and brought heavy fire to bear when needed. (Navy)

In conjunction with the Vietnamese Marines, the Marine Special Landing Force (SLF) carried out Operation DECKHOUSE V, a landing in the Mekong Delta. Due to security leaks, the main force VC unit which was in the area was able to escape and results were extremely disappointing. Two H-34s pass over an LVTH-6 armed with a 105mm howitzer during the operation. (USMC via Bell)

Charging the jungle hideout of a sniper, a Marine sprays the brush with his M16. Heavy jungle such as this made excellent cover for the enemy and detection was extremely difficult. (USMC)

Heavy concentrations of NVA made the northern portions of South Vietnam a hot spot through most of the war. Marines return enemy fire in heavy jungle growth during a mission around Phu Bai. (USMC)

Members of the 1st ARVN Division, the best of the South Vietnamese Army regular units, jump from a H-34 during a joint USMC/ARVN mission near the DMZ. When well led and supported, the ARVN troops could fight extremely well. These qualities were often missing, leading to a very disappointing performance on the part of the Vietnamese troops. (USMC)

Troops of the South Korean Capital (Tiger) Division search a bunker near Qui Nhon. The ROKs were often brutal when confronted with opposition and used extreme means to pacify an area on more than one occasions.

Sloshing through a stream, a young Marine carries part of a mortar in addition to his own equipment. It was common practice for a squad or platoon to divide up such equipment among its members along with extra ammo so that the unit could be self-supporting in the initial stages of a fire-fight. (USMC)

As part of the "Psy War" approach to gaining "Chieu Hoi's," loudspeakers were used to broadcast appeals to surrender prior to a battle. This grunt from the 35th Infantry carries part of the loudspeaker system on his back in addition to his regular gear. Results varied, but enough defectors did come over that the program was kept active. (Army)

A member of the 101st Screaming Eagles hangs out belts of M60 ammunition to dry during Operation WHEELER. Excessive dirt on the ammo belts could cause the gun to jam, although the M60 was nowhere near as prone to jam as the M16. (Army)

As the year came to an end the Marines were still under heavy pressure up north. A reconnaissance patrol moves along a trail looking for NVA. All of the patrol members wear soft covers rather than helmets and carry a lot of extra equipment. (USMC)

Marines string barbed wire to increase their fixed defenses around their perimeter. With air and artillery support the Marines felt they could handle any attack the NVA threw at them. (USMC)

Christmas in any war zone is not a happy time but this Marine carries a small tree as a reminder of better times to come as he prepares to leave on a patrol around Con Thien, one of the major hot spots in the northern provinces during 1967. (USMC)

An increase in enemy activity in the Khe Sanh area caused a great deal of worry in the US high command and in Washington. Steps were taken to beef up the defenses there to prevent the NVA from gaining a Dien Bien Phu type victory over the Marines. An M48A3 and an "Ontos" sit near the perimeter to provide fire support for the entrenched Marines at the base. (USMC)

Preparations

By the early Summer of 1967, the communist leadership in Hanoi had come to the conclusion that the war was not going in their favor. Although not defeated, their forces were on the defensive throughout South Vietnam and American strength was on the rise. In the U.S., the hoped for anti-war effort had not sufficiently materialized to erode public support for the government's Vietnam policy. From near collapse in 1965, the South Vietnamese government and its armed forces had rebound and, although still shaky, were becoming progressively stronger each day. If the war continued at its current pace, the communists would eventually lose.

Out of this realization came a both daring and desperate plan. The communist leaders decided to carry out a nation wide offensive over the 1968 Tet holiday to hit all vital allied installations. They hoped this attack could achieve some, if not all, of these goals: (1) cause unrest in the populated areas; (2) inflict a series of defeats on allied units; (3) split the alliance between the U.S. and South Vietnam; (4) start a general uprising among the people and; (5) demonstrate that the war was far from won, fueling the anti-war sentiment in the U.S. To carry this out, their forces in the south would have to plan, organize and bring in supplies for units across the whole length of the country and coordinate the entire undertaking with split second timing.

Beginning in late Summer, large amounts of weapons, ammunition and other supplies began to flow into the cities and towns targeted for the attack. Every conceivable method possible was utilized, including fake funerals where the coffins were filled with arms, then buried in cemeteries to be dug up just before the attack. Throughout the Fall this effort continued, without any detection by South Vietnamese authorities. Numerous Viet Cong units also began to filter into position, linking up with VC cadre within the cities to plan out their various attacks.

In order to mask the infiltration of men and materials, the communists also launched a series of attacks in the Fall by NVA regulars along the border areas. These "border battles" were designed to lure American units away from the population centers and put them out of position for a quick response once the attack began. In addition, it was hoped the battles would cause intelligence to focus on these areas and overlook any possible information which might leak out about the actual attack. The culmination of this effort was the isolation and siege of the Marine base at Khe Sanh in northern I Corps. Almost all the American attention was focused on this tiny base as over 30,000 NVA moved in around it, fueling fears that they might try to achieve a Dien Bien Phu type victory.

Despite these moves and all attempts at secrecy, some evidence that something was up filtered down to American and South Vietnamese intelligence. The apparent lack of purpose or direction by enemy forces during the "border battles" made intelligence personnel look into communist motives. Some information was captured indicating a possible series of small suicide like attacks designed more to cause embarrassment and an upheaval rather than to gain any worthwhile military objectives. By December, this was revised as information came in indicating that the VC and NVA might try some sort of limited attack to upset the allied momentum. More evidence in support of this, including documents and prisoners, was captured in January of 1968 less than a month before the Tet holidays, prompting some readjustment of U.S. and allied forces. But the focus of American attention still rested on Khe Sanh in I Corps, where over half of the U.S. combat battalions were stationed to counter the communist buildup.

Unfortunately, despite the numerous warnings, ARVN and American leaders never suspected just how widespread the communist offensive would be. No one really believed the communists could organize, supply and coordinate a country wide assault and, even if they could, such an attack would be speedily crushed by allied forces. It would achieve no military goals, while at the same time bring high casualties to the enemy. Logically, from a military standpoint, they were correct about the latter portion, but failed to appreciate that the enemy could lay out such an offensive. Their most serious error, however, was in failing to see that the political goals of such an offensive, superseded the military achievements. This failure to correctly gauge the communist capability and goals were to have widespread repercussion in the weeks and months ahead. As the Tet holiday approached, a festive air began to take hold across South Vietnam.

No one believed the enemy would carry out any attacks over this sacred period of time, for Tet was like a combination Christmas and New Years to the Vietnamese, both north and south. American units were placed on alert, but nearly half of all ARVN forces were given leave for Tet, despite U.S. misgivings. As ARVN troops left their compounds and base for home, they mingled with many of their countrymen in the streets of various South Vietnamese cities, towns and villages. Unknown to them was the fact that many of the men and women they came in contact with were Viet Cong on their way to a secret rendezvous of arms caches in preparations for the communist offensive. As the end of January drew near, small groups began to position themselves around key bases, installations and civilian targets in anticipation of the greatest offensive yet launched in the Indochina War.

Just prior to Tet, the VC began to move into the cities by a variety of means. To bring in weapons they even staged fake funerals with the coffins filled with weapons which were to be dug up just before the attack. Perhaps this funeral procession which is going past an American column was one of these. (Army)

The Tet Offensive

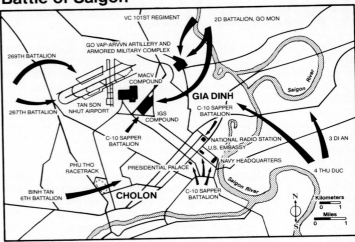

Battle of Saigon

The initial communist attacks began in the early hours of 30 January at Nha Trang in II Corps, a day ahead of the main VC assault. Whether this was by design or accident is still not known, even today. This was followed by a number of scattered rocket and ground attacks against several military installations and towns. Though some ARVN Commanders placed their men on alert, most refused to believe there was a serious threat and did not recall soldiers on leave or increase their security precautions. American units, already alerted, waited, unaware of the onslaught which they would soon face.

Shortly after midnight on 31 January, the communists launched their all out offensive across all of South Vietnam. In Saigon, numerous groups of infiltrators, led by Saigon natives, hit the Presidential Palace, military installations, key civilian buildings and the U.S. Embassy. The embassy attack, despite its military insignificance, captured world attention due to sensational coverage by the news media. Lightly defended, the few Marine guards and MPs were able to prevent the VC from entering the embassy itself, although they did get onto the compound grounds. Within seven hours all the guerrillas had been either killed or captured by Marine Security Guards (MSGs) and Army MPs but the attack was totally blown out of proportion by the media in its quest for sensationalism.

Throughout the rest of Saigon and across the country it was much the same: small bands of Viet Cong made some initial gains due to stealth and surprise. In many cases this initial success quickly turned to disaster as American and ARVN forces quickly counter-attacked. In numerous areas, however, reinforcements were able to link up with the smaller groups and dig in. In other areas larger enemy forces moved into position from the surrounding country-side and seized key areas. These units, well armed and supplied, proved much harder to dislodge and severe fighting resulted. In Saigon, enemy forces moved into Cholon, the Chinese sector, and established several strong points. To root them out eventually required close air support from USAF and VNAF aircraft, along with armor and artillery support. It took over two weeks for Americans and South Vietnamese forces to finally secure the area, which was almost totally devastated by the fierce fighting.

Further north, the communists were able to capture a large part of Hue, the former imperial capital and present provincial capital of Thuc Thien. Although the headquarters of the 1st ARVN division, one of the best South Vietnamese units, and surrounded by numerous Marine units, the VC were able to quickly achieve their objectives since the majority of the allied forces were deployed in support of the besieged Khe Sanh garrison or in the countryside to keep open lines of communication. Those units still inside the city quickly rallied and within a few hours both ARVN and Marine units were moving to dislodge the enemy. Unfortunately, these initial moves were unable to drive out the entrenched VC who were deeply dug in, though numerous isolated allied positions were relieved. Both sides rushed in reinforcements until twenty allied battalions and the equivalent of a VC division were committed in and around the city.

Early in the fighting the job of recapturing the southern part of the city was given to the Marines while the ARVN assumed respon-sibility for the Citadel across the river, a thick walled fortress ideal for defense. From the beginning the fighting was fierce, since the enemy had to be driven out of each house in vicious street fighting. Backed by aircraft, naval gunfire support, armor and artillery, the allies slowly ground the enemy down, but in the process Hue was almost totally destroyed. By the end of February, the final VC positions were finally taken, ending the month long battle. Nearly 3,800 allied personnel were killed or wounded while over 5,000 communists were killed along with untold wounded. While in control of Hue, the communist also murdered thousands of people, mainly captured government workers, officials and soldiers, along with foreign nationals in some of the worst atrocities of the entire war. This planned slaughter also occurred in other cities as the communists sought to purge the country of any opposition to their rule. By comparison, such incidents as the My Lai massacre (March 1968) were isolated occurrences but received far more press coverage than the brutal extermination practiced during Tet by the communists.

By early March, stability on the battlefield had been achieved as the allied forces eliminated the last vestiges of the enemy offensive. By conservative estimates the communists had over 20,000 men killed and between 30-40,000 wounded, including the majority of the Viet Cong. Allied losses, while heavy, were nowhere near this, and American and ARVN forces quickly moved onto the counter-offensive across the country to take advantage of the enemies losses.

Unfortunately, however, biased press coverage portrayed Tet as a communist victory, despite these huge losses in men. While the offensive had indeed been well planned out and executed, it achieved

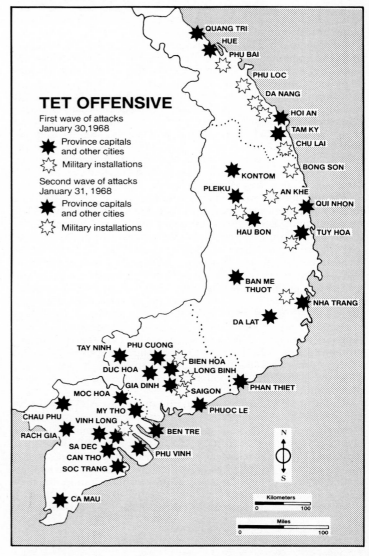

TET OFFENSIVE

First wave of attacks
January 30, 1968

★ Province capitals and other cities

☆ Military installations

Second wave of attacks
January 31, 1968

★ Province capitals and other cities

☆ Military installations

Enemy Attack on Hue
January 31, 1968

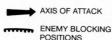
- ➡ AXIS OF ATTACK
- 〜 ENEMY BLOCKING POSITIONS
- ⟡ ALLIED DEFENSE PERIMETERS

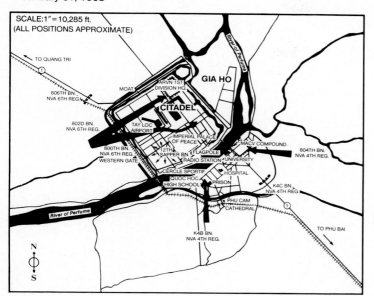

SCALE: 1" = 10,285 ft.
(ALL POSITIONS APPROXIMATE)

TO QUANG TRI
806TH BN. NVA 6TH REG.
MOAT
ARVN 1ST DIVISION HQ
GIA HO
River of Perfume
CITADEL
802D BN. NVA 6TH REG.
TAY LOC AIRPORT
IMPERIAL PALACE OF PEACE
MACV COMPOUND
800TH BN. NVA 6TH REG. WESTERN GATE
12TH SAPPER BN
FLAGPOLE
RADIO STATION
UNIVERSITY
804TH BN. NVA 4TH REG.
CERCLE SPORTIF
HOSPITAL
QUOC HOC HIGH SCHOOL
PRISON
K4C BN. NVA 4TH REG.
PHU CAM CATHEDRAL
River of Perfume
TO PHU BAI
K4B BN. NVA 4TH REG.
N S

Hue: The Allied Counterattack

- ➡ AXIS OF ATTACK
- 〜 ALLIED BLOCKING POSITIONS
- ⟡ ENEMY DEFENSE PERIMETERS
- ▦ COMMUNIST-CONTROLLED AREAS

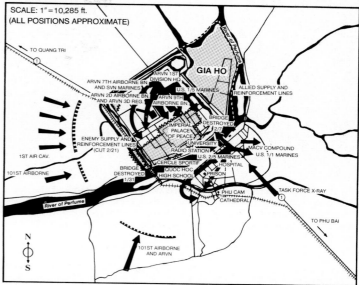

SCALE: 1" = 10,285 ft.
(ALL POSITIONS APPROXIMATE)

TO QUANG TRI
ARVN 7TH AIRBORNE BN. AND SVN MARINES
ARVN 1ST DIVISION HQ
GIA HO
ARVN 2D AIRBORNE BN. AND ARVN 3D REG.
U.S. 1/5 MARINES
ARVN 9TH AIRBORNE BN.
ALLIED SUPPLY AND REINFORCEMENT LINES
BRIDGE DESTROYED 2/7
IMPERIAL PALACE OF PEACE
ENEMY SUPPLY AND REINFORCEMENT LINES (CUT 2/21)
UNIVERSITY
RADIO STATION
MACV COMPOUND
1ST AIR CAV.
CERCLE SPORTIF
U.S. 2/5 MARINES
HOSPITAL
U.S. 1/1 MARINES
101ST AIRBORNE
BRIDGE DESTROYED 1/31
QUOC HOC HIGH SCHOOL
PRISON
River of Perfume
PHU CAM CATHEDRAL
TASK FORCE X-RAY
TO PHU BAI
101ST AIRBORNE AND ARVN
N S

no significant military gains, a fact conveniently overlooked by the news media. In the final analysis, Tet was born of desperation, like the German offensive in 1944 known as the "Battle of the Bulge." The media, for the most part, chose to ignore that fact, and concentrated more on the mistakes made by American and ARVN officials in failing to detect this communist buildup. The end result for the enemy was a moral, psychological and political victory due to this coverage. Within a short time President Johnson would announce his refusal to run for reelection, and this, along with Tet, helped fuel the anti-war movement, exactly as the North Vietnamese had hoped.

An Air Force Air Policeman examines the body of a Viet Cong infiltrator who was killed trying to gain access to Tan Son Nhut Air Base. (USAF)

One of the initial targets of the surprise attack was the American Embassy in Saigon. It was chosen for its political and psychological impact, rather than any military reasons. Although the assault team managed to get onto the grounds, they never penetrated the embassy itself due to the bravery of the guards. All were captured or killed within a few hours, such as this one who lies dead on the grounds. (Army)

During the initial stages of the attack a truckload of MPs were dispatched to a trouble spot but were caught in an ambush along a narrow street and wiped out. The next day these troops secured the scene and recovered the truck and the bodies of their comrades. (Army)

At Tan Son Nhut airport security police killed a large number of attackers, although some did manage to penetrate the base. Security Police (SPs) examine documents found on the bodies of a group of infiltrators who were spotted and killed before they could do any harm. (USAF)

Some of the heaviest fighting took place around the "Y" bridge in the southern part of Saigon. Troops from the 9th Infantry Division fire on dug-in VC near the bridge. During this battle there was a great deal of house-to-house fighting. (Army)

The Phu Tho race track, a major VC strong point, was located near Tan Son Nhut airport. These ARVN soldiers watch as an RTO calls in artillery fire on the enemy position. (Army)

A soldier runs for cover during the street fighting in Saigon. Troops used to jungle fighting had to quickly adapt to the changes brought about in this type of urban warfare. (Army)

The Chinese suburb of Cholon was the site of heavy fighting as the VC dug in and had to be rooted out house by house. An ARVN Ranger takes a sniper under fire while other Rangers try to get into a better position. The Rangers were some of the best ARVN troops and performed very well during Tet. (Army)

During the fighting, the Marines had to be watchful for enemy infiltrators who would slip into supposedly cleared areas and ambush the Marines. These Marines take cover behind a jeep and truck during one such attack. (USMC)

Although fighting raged across the entire country, the most severe fighting was in Hue, the old Imperial Capital. In Hue the Marines were engaged in a savage contest with the dug-in enemy. These Marines move through a damaged house during the bitter fighting. (USMC)

All types of weapons were brought to bear against the dug in enemy. This M67 flame thrower tank covers a destroyed bridge near the end of the battle Tanks were invaluable in providing support during the heavy street fighting. (USMC)

These Marines bring their 106MM recoilless rifle to bear on a VC strong point. The 106 was very effective in this type of fighting since its flat trajectory allowed for pinpoint accuracy against very small targets. (USMC)

In the final analysis, though, it was the individual Marine who made the difference. This Marine sniper scans the building in the background for signs of enemy movement. (USMC)

A wounded Marine is carried in a poncho by his buddies to an aide station for evacuation. Casualties during the house-to-house fighting were high, rivaling any other battle the Marines fought in Vietnam. (USMC)

Marines scan the area through an opening in a wall for signs of enemy activity. Such walls provided ideal cover and protection for the enemy, making it necessary to use heavy firepower to dig him out. (USMC)

The end result was the destruction of one of the most beautiful cities in South Vietnam. After the fighting, when the communists were finally driven out at the end of February, most of the city lay in ruins. (USMC)

Khe Sanh

After the first Marine sweep around the Khe Sanh area in early 1966, they did not return to the plateau until October of 1966 during operation PRAIRIE. A single battalion moved into the base, displacing the Special Forces camp which moved about six miles down Colonial Route 9 (CR9) from the camp. The battalion remained there until February of 1967 when it was replaced by a single company. When heavy fighting developed near Hill 861 (the number indicated height above sea level in meters. If two hills were the same elevation, a letter indicating direction was added - example 881N, 881S) more were flown in, but were withdrawn after the battle was over.

The base, though linked by CR 9, could only be supplied by air since the road was in a serious state of disrepair and had many potential ambush sites. A small dirt airstrip had been improved in the Summer of 1966 by a Navy Mobile Construction Battalion (Seebees). Some artillery was also deployed in support of the defenders, while 175 MM guns located at Camp Carroll and the Rockpile could provide additional firepower on short notice.

The Marines, along with the CIDG, a Marines Combined Action Company (CAC) and their Regional Force (RF) Company located in the village of Khe Sanh monitored a key infiltration route from Laos into Quang Tri province. The Marines did not want to really keep a garrison force in the area but under pressure from GEN Westmoreland this was more or less forced down their throats. He wanted the plateau secured as a possible jumping off point for an invasion into Laos to cut the Ho Chi Minh trail, in addition to hampering communist infiltration.

The first major NVA attempt to overrun the base occurred in late April of 1967 when a Marine patrol prematurely set off an enemy assault when it encountered NVA troops on Hill 861. Reinforcements were rushed in and heavy fighting quickly developed for control of the hills overlooking the base. The "hill fights" continued into May as the Marines fought against prepared NVA positions on Hills 861, 881N and 881S. When the NVA finally pulled back they left behind close to 1,000 dead but for the Marines the price had also been high with over 150 men lost. Following this vicious fighting, enemy activity dropped off except for a short period of time in mid-June. During this lull the airfield was closed in mid-August and resurfaced with crushed rock to improve its ability to handle heavy traffic. It was reopened in October and this improvement was later to be extremely significant in keeping the base resupplied during the siege.

In late 1967, increased enemy activity in the area resulted in additional Marine reinforcements being rushed into the base. By the end of December there was enough evidence to indicate that the NVA might attempt a "Dien Bien Phu" battle against the Marines in order to gain a major victory. This was reinforced when five high ranking North Vietnamese officers were killed while reconnoitering the Khe Sanh perimeter. In addition, intelligence reports showed that two, and possibly three, NVA divisions were in the immediate vicinity of the base. Coupled with the increased enemy activity, the possibilities of the North Vietnamese going all out for a major victory over the Marines assumed terrifying potential.

The Battle for Khe Sanh

By mid-January, the Marines are in almost daily contact with NVA forces, either in patrol actions, ground sweeps or through attacks on their perimeter. Additionally heavy mortar, artillery and rocket attacks hit the base, destroying the main ammo dump and numerous other installations and bunkers. On 21 January, the communists attempted to take Khe Sanh village southwest of the base but after heavy fighting were driven off by the defenders and support fire from Khe Sanh. Due to its exposed position, however, the village was then abandoned and the defenders were either incorporated into the base defenses or evacuated with their families. To further strengthen the camp an ARVN Ranger battalion was flown in and air support was coordinated under Operation NIAGARA to provide a literal waterfall of bombs around the base to ensure its survival.

Khe Sanh

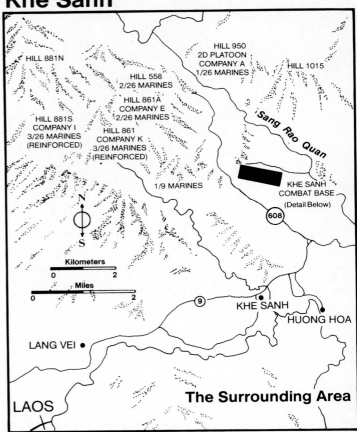

The Surrounding Area

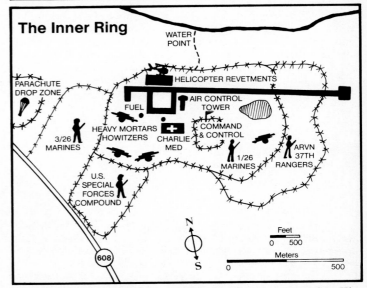

The Inner Ring

While the focus of Washington and Saigon was centered on Khe Sanh, the communists launched their nation-wide Tet Offensive on 30 January. Believed by some to be a cover to divert attention and forces from Khe Sanh, this attack caused widespread confusion throughout the country as allied forces rush to recapture towns, villages and cities seized by the VC and NVA. Some officials later suggest that the siege of the base was a ruse to draw attention away from preparations for Tet and that the North Vietnamese never seriously considering attacking the base. The truth will probably never be known since the communists version of what actually happened will never be known, based on their known practice of rewriting history to justify their own position.

During the first week in February the NVA carried out two major attacks in the area: one against the base and the other against the CIDG camp at Lang Vei. For a short period of time they gained a foothold in the perimeter but were driven out by a Marine counterattack, losing over 100 men, against seven Marine dead. At the CIDG camp, however, it was a different story. Supported by nine PT-76 light tanks, an NVA battalion from the 304th Division struck the camp. It fell despite heavy support fire and efforts by the camp defenders. Some survivors were able to make it out of the camp and these were either picked up by Marine helicopters or walked back to the fire base. The Khe Sanh commander, fearing infiltration, would not let the indigenous personnel stay in the camp and they were either evacuated or returned to their homes in the jungle.

The day following the fall of Lang Vei, 8 February, an NVA battalion made the first daylight attack on the base, but this was repulsed with over 150 dead. Two weeks later, another attack was carried out, this time against the ARVN Ranger position, being easily repulsed with the help of artillery fire. This period, following the onslaught of the Tet offensive, marked the formal "seige" period for the base. Throughout February and into March the communists subject Khe Sanh to a hail of mortar, artillery and rocket fire, with over 1,000 shells impacting daily on the base. In addition, the North Vietnamese began to construct trench systems around the base, similar to the ones used at Dien Bien Phu fourteen years earlier. No more major ground assaults occurred and fighting was confined to patrol actions in the immediate vicinity of the base.

By mid-March, despite intense shelling, intelligence reports began to indicate that the NVA troops are starting to withdraw from the area, although the heavy shelling continues. Plans are made to relieve the base with Marine and Army elements moving east in conjunction with a Marine breakout from the base itself. The opening moves of Operation PEGASUS started in late March and on 1 April ground and airmobile assaults opened the attack. While elements of the 1st Cav and 101st Airborne secured numerous LZs, Marines and ARVN troops pushed down CR 9. Despite some resistance, the allied force moved forward fairly quickly and on 8 April, Army elements linked-up with the Marines in Khe Sanh. By the middle of the month the road to the base was open, resulting in the termination of Operation PEGASUS. Within two months, orders went out for the dismantling of the base, due in part to the additional Army airmobile assets which had moved into the area, along with newer fire support bases which had been constructed in the region. By the end of June, nothing remained of the base, and it quickly fell into the pages of history.

At Khe Sanh the Marines prepared for the NVA ground attack which they felt for sure would come. Initially, the airfield was able to receive incoming flights but enemy fire later made this too dangerous, destroying a number of aircraft including this USAF C-123. (USAF)

The cost of the battle in human terms was never accurately figured out. Official Marines casualties during the seige number 205 killed but if all American casualties associated with the battle, (Long Vei, Khe Sanh village, relief operations, etc) were counted, the figure is almost double. For the North Vietnamese, intelligence estimates that between 10,000 to 15,000 enemy soldiers were lost during the campaign, mainly to supporting fire. It is highly unlikely that the actual number will ever be known, but even if the figures are in error by half, the numbers are still substantial. Whether or not Khe Sanh was the actual objective of the North Vietnamese or a clever ploy to attract attention, the fact remains that they paid a high price for whatever they were able to achieve. In the final analysis the Marines who defended the area never gave in, despite what was thrown at them, showing the world the true worth of the American fighting man in time of adversity.

For a time supplies were parachuted into the base by low flying transports. This C-130 is making a low altitude paradrop to the Marines at the main base. The steep angle of the drop kept the supplies within a small area. (USMC via Bell)

For the most part the Marines based at Khe Sanh lived below ground during the siege. These positions were part of the defenses of "C" Company of the 26th Regiment. (USMC)

Heavy firepower was available to defend the base in case of a major assault. This 105MM howitzer, stationed at the base, fires on NVA positions in the hills near the camp. Additional artillery was available for support from other fire bases to the east of the camp. (USMC)

Marines train members of the Regional Force in the use of various weapons including the Browning .50 caliber air cooled machine gun, M60 7.62MM machine and M16 rifles. The commander at Kha Sanh later ordered all RF personnel to be evacuated from the base. (Reuben Garcia)

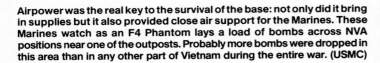

Airpower was the real key to the survival of the base: not only did it bring in supplies but it also provided close air support for the Marines. These Marines watch as an F4 Phantom lays a load of bombs across NVA positions near one of the outposts. Probably more bombs were dropped in this area than in any other part of Vietnam during the entire war. (USMC)

This CH-46 Seahorse helicopter was destroyed on the ground by enemy shell fire. Resupply missions into the base were very dangerous for both the aircrews and the men unloading the helicopters and transports. (Reuben Garcia)

With the Tet Offensive smashed, the overland relief of Khe Sanh got underway 1 April. Code-named Operation PEGASUS it was a combined air-ground assault by the 1st Cav and the Marines. (USMC)

The ground assault had to replace numerous destroyed bridges as it moved overland and the quickest way was to use a tank launched bridge ing equipment and moved down Colonial Route 9 toward Khe Sanh. (USMC)

A Marine fires a 60MM mortar against NVA positions during the relief of Khe Sanh. Rather than set up the bipod which goes with it he is using his hands to steady it. Some troops became very proficient at this and were surprisingly accurate using this method. (USMC)

The 1st Cav, in conjunction with the Marine ground drive, made a series of airmobile assaults to trap the NVA. Using a backhoe, these cavalrymen prepare fortifications at an FSB during the drive. The howitzer in the background is one of the new lightweight guns with a longer range. (Army)

Epilogue

The Tet Offensive and the seige of Khe Sanh marked a turning point in the Vietnam War for the United States. Though the communists suffered a major military defeat during this period, they were to garner a tremendous political victory from this action. The media quickly keyed in on certain aspects of the attack such as the incident at the embassy which, although sensational in terms of headlines, meant little in the overall course of events.

Unfortunately, this type of reporting, while great copy, was inaccurate and failed to present the facts in a clear and concise way. As a result the American people got a very slanted picture of events. By comparison the massacre of innocent South Vietnamese in Hue and other cities was almost totally glossed over by the press. Had the news media been as quick to show this side of the communist offensive along with the valor of the American and allied soldiers during the offensive, a much truer picture of events would have been the outcome.

As a result of the anti-war reporting, the American people, already weary of the war, began to question it in a far more serious vein. While there were indeed things which needed to be examined, both with respect to Tet and the general war effort, a calm, rational examination was not possible due to the circumstances. Within a few months President Johnson would announce that he was not a candidate for re-election, a new commander of US forces would replace GEN Westmoreland, and the anti-war movement would begin a concerted drive to end American involvement in the war. These were to be the actual results of Tet and as the last smoke from the offensive cleared away, U.S. Soldiers, Sailors, Marines and Airmen began to realize that changes were coming and there was little they could do to influence these events. As 1968 approached Spring, subtle but noticeable changes within the war effort were taking place which will be covered the the last part of the American involvement in Vietnam.